Getting Started with Processing.py

Allison Parrish, Ben Fry, and Casey Reas

SAN FRANCISCO, CA

Getting Started with Processing.py

by Allison Parrish, Ben Fry, and Casey Reas

Published by Maker Media, Inc., 1160 Battery Street East, Suite 125, San Francisco, CA 94111.

Maker Media books may be purchased for educational, business, or sales promotional use. Online editions are also available for most titles (*http://safaribookson-line.com*). For more information, contact O'Reilly Media's institutional sales department: 800-998-9938 or *corporate@oreilly.com*.

Editor: Patrick Di Justo
Production Editor: Nicholas Adams
Copyeditor: Jasmine Kwityn
Proofreader: Gillian McGarvey

Indexer: Angela Howard
Interior Designer: David Futato
Cover Designer: Karen Montgomery
Illustrator: Rebecca Demarest

May 2016:   First Edition

Revision History for the First Edition

2016-05-06:   First Release

See *http://oreilly.com/catalog/errata.csp?isbn=9781457186837* for release details.

978-1-457-18683-7

[LSI]

Contents

Preface

Processing.py is an interactive programming and graphics framework for the Python programming language. Jonathan Feinberg created Processing.py in 2010, basing his work on an existing programming framework called Processing, created by Casey Reas and Ben Fry in 2001. Casey and Ben were inspired by how simple it was to write interesting programs with the languages of their childhood (Logo and BASIC), and intended their framework to be a way to sketch (prototype) full-screen, interactive software without the frustration of languages typically used for this purpose at the time (C++ and Java).

When the Processing project was first created, it was intended to be a language-agnostic, arts-oriented approach to interactive programming, taking inspiration from OpenGL, PostScript, and Design By Numbers, among other sources. Although early versions of Processing were compatible with the Python programming language, a decision was made to focus the team's limited resources on a Java-based syntax. Jonathan Feinberg's Processing.py project restored Python compatibility to the project. (For more information on the relationship between Processing, Processing.py, and Python, see Appendix E.)

Processing was designed to be an ideal environment for teaching design and art students how to program and to give more technical students an easier way to work with graphics. The combination is a positive departure from the way programming is usually taught and, since 2001, Processing has been at the center of a growing movement to promote software literacy in the visual arts and visual literacy within technology.

I'm a strong believer in the power of the Python programming language and have taught Python with great success to novice programmers in many disciplines, from software engineering to the humanities to the arts. For this reason, I was overjoyed when Casey and Ben approached me to help write this book, which brings together their time-tested creative coding framework with a programming language I've found so friendly and productive for novice coders and experts alike. We believe that Processing.py is not just a great framework for learning how to program but an invaluable addition to the toolbox of Python programmers of all stripes who need a simple and clear means of making interactive applications.

This book is available in three slightly different versions. One version is an introduction to Processing using its traditional, Java-based syntax, and a second covers p5.js, a version of Processing reinterpreted for today's Web. The version you now have in your possession introduces Processing with the Python programming language, using Processing.py as the bridge between the two. The three books are organized in very similar ways, and much of the content is identical from one book to the other. The main difference, of course, is that the code examples in this book are all written in Python. This book also contains some additional information and educational material about Python-specific techniques, idioms, and data structures. We believe this book will work well as an introductory text for the Processing Development Environment, the Python programming language, and interactive programming in general.

We hope you'll have fun with this book and be inspired to continue programming. Let's begin!

How This Book Is Organized

The chapters in this book are organized as follows:

- 1/Hello: Learn about Processing.py.
- 2/Starting to Code: Create your first Processing.py program.
- 3/Draw: Define and draw simple shapes.
- 4/Variables: Store, modify, and reuse data.
- 5/Response: Control and influence programs with the mouse and the keyboard.
- 6/Translate, Rotate, Scale: Transform the coordinates.
- 7/Media: Load and display media, including images, fonts, and vector files.
- 8/Motion: Move and choreograph shapes.
- 9/Functions: Build new code modules.
- 10/Objects: Create code modules that combine variables and functions.
- 11/Lists: Simplify working with lists of variables.
- 12/Data and Dictionaries: Load and visualize data using the dictionary data structure.
- 13/Extend: Learn about sound, PDF export, and reading data from an Arduino board.

Who This Book Is For

This book is written for people who want a casual and concise introduction to computer programming so that they can create images and simple interactive programs. It's especially suited to beginning programmers who want to learn the Python programming language. *Getting Started with Processing.py* is not a programming textbook; as the title suggests, it will get you started. It's for teenagers, hobbyists, grandparents, and everyone in between.

This book is also appropriate for people with programming experience, particularly in the Python programming language, who want to learn the basics of interactive computer graphics. *Getting Started with Processing.py* contains techniques that can be applied to creating games, animation, and interfaces.

Conventions Used in This Book

The following typographical conventions are used in this book:

Italic

Indicates new terms, URLs, email addresses, filenames, and file extensions.

`Constant width`

Used for program listings, as well as within paragraphs to refer to program elements such as variable or function names, databases, data types, environment variables, statements, and keywords.

`Constant width italic`

Shows text that should be replaced with user-supplied values or by values determined by context.

 This type of paragraph signifies a general note.

 This element indicates a warning or caution.

Using Code Examples

This book is here to help you get your job done. In general, you may use the code in this book in your programs and documentation. You do not need to contact us for permission unless you're reproducing a significant portion of the code. For example, writing a program that uses several chunks of code from this book does not require permission. Selling or distributing a

CD-ROM of examples from *Make:* books does require permission. Answering a question by citing this book and quoting example code does not require permission. Incorporating a significant amount of example code from this book into your product's documentation does require permission.

We appreciate, but do not require, attribution. An attribution usually includes the title, author, publisher, and ISBN. For example: "*Make: Getting Started with Processing.py* by Allison Parrish, Ben Fry, and Casey Reas. Copyright 2016 Maker Media, Inc., 978-1-457-18683-7."

If you feel your use of code examples falls outside fair use or the permission given here, feel free to contact us at permissions@oreilly.com.

Safari® Books Online

Safari Books Online is an on-demand digital library that delivers expert content in both book and video form from the world's leading authors in technology and business.

Technology professionals, software developers, web designers, and business and creative professionals use Safari Books Online as their primary resource for research, problem solving, learning, and certification training.

Safari Books Online offers a range of plans and pricing for enterprise, government, education, and individuals.

Members have access to thousands of books, training videos, and prepublication manuscripts in one fully searchable database from publishers like Maker Media, O'Reilly Media, Prentice Hall Professional, Addison-Wesley Professional, Microsoft Press, Sams, Que, Peachpit Press, Focal Press, Cisco Press, John Wiley & Sons, Syngress, Morgan Kaufmann, IBM Redbooks, Packt, Adobe Press, FT Press, Apress, Manning, New Riders, McGraw-Hill, Jones & Bartlett, Course Technology, and hundreds more. For more information about Safari Books Online, please visit us online.

How to Contact Us

Please address comments and questions concerning this book to the publisher:

Maker Media, Inc.
1160 Battery Street East, Suite 125
San Francisco, California 94111
800-998-9938 (in the United States or Canada)
http://makermedia.com/contact-us/

Make: unites, inspires, informs, and entertains a growing community of resourceful people who undertake amazing projects in their backyards, basements, and garages. *Make:* celebrates your right to tweak, hack, and bend any technology to your will. The *Make:* audience continues to be a growing culture and community that believes in bettering ourselves, our environment, our educational system—our entire world. This is much more than an audience, it's a worldwide movement that *Make:* is leading—we call it the Maker Movement.

For more information about *Make:*, visit us online:

Make: magazine: http://makezine.com/magazine/
Maker Faire: http://makerfaire.com
Makezine.com: http://makezine.com
Maker Shed: http://makershed.com/

Acknowledgments

We thank Brian Jepson, Anna Kaziunas France, and Patrick DiJusto for their great energy, support, and insight.

We can't imagine this book without Massimo Banzi's *Getting Started with Arduino* (Maker Media). Massimo's excellent book is the prototype.

A small group of individuals has, for years, contributed essential time and energy to Processing. Dan Shiffman is our partner in the Processing Foundation, the 501(c)(3) organization that supports the Processing software. Much of the core code for Processing 2.0 and 3.0 has come from the sharp minds of Andrés

Colubri and Manindra Moharana. Scott Murray, Jamie Kosoy, and Jon Gacnik have built a wonderful web infrastructure for the project. James Grady is rocking the 3.0 user interface. We thank Florian Jenett for his years of diverse work on the project, including the forums, website, and design. Elie Zananiri and Andreas Schlegel have created the infrastructure for building and documenting contributed libraries, and have spent countless hours curating the lists. Many others have contributed significantly to the project; the precise data is available at https:// github.com/processing.

This book grew out of teaching with Processing at UCLA. Chandler McWilliams has been instrumental in defining these classes. Casey thanks the undergraduate students in the Department of Design Media Arts at UCLA for their energy and enthusiasm. His teaching assistants have been great collaborators in defining how Processing is taught. Hats off to Tatsuya Saito, John Houck, Tyler Adams, Aaron Siegel, Casey Alt, Andrés Colubri, Michael Kontopoulos, David Elliot, Christo Allegra, Pete Hawkes, and Lauren McCarthy.

Jonathan Feinberg began developing Processing.py independently in 2010. Google provided initial support for the development of Python Mode for the Processing IDE in April 2014. The Processing Foundation and Fathom provided additional logistical support. James Gilles made important contributions to the development of Python Mode as well. Work on the *Reference*, examples, and tutorials was funded in the summer of 2014 in part by the Integrative Design, Arts, and Technology (IDeATe) initiative at Carnegie Mellon University, and by a grant from the National Endowment for the Arts managed by the Frank-Ratchye STUDIO for Creative Inquiry at CMU. Thank you to Miles Peyton for his work on the documentation and to Golan Levin for guidance and support. We also thank Luca Damasco, who helped bring Processing.py into alignment with the newly released Processing 3 during the 2015 Google Summer of Code, again under guidance from Golan Levin and the Frank-Ratchye STUDIO for Creative Inquiry at CMU.

The Processing.py project is currently maintained by Jonathan Feinberg and a small team of contributors. You can learn more about Processing.py at the project's website (*http://py.process ing.org/*).

Through founding the Aesthetics and Computation Group (1996–2002) at the MIT Media Lab, John Maeda made all of this possible.

1/Hello

Processing is for writing software to make images, animations, and interactions. The idea is to write a single line of code and have a circle show up on the screen. Add a few more lines of code, and the circle follows the mouse. Another line of code, and the circle changes color when the mouse is pressed. We call this *sketching* with code. You write one line, then add another, then another, and so on. The result is a program created one piece at a time.

Programming courses typically focus on structure and theory first. Anything visual—an interface, an animation—is considered a dessert to be enjoyed only after finishing your vegetables, usually after several weeks of studying algorithms and methods. Over the years, we've watched many friends try to take such courses and drop out after the first lecture or after a long, frustrating night before the first assignment deadline. What initial curiosity they had about making the computer work for them was lost because they couldn't see a path from what they had to learn first to what they wanted to create.

Processing offers a way to learn programming through creating interactive graphics. There are many possible ways to teach coding, but students often find encouragement and motivation in immediate visual feedback. Processing's capacity for providing that feedback has made it a popular way to approach programming, and its emphasis on images, sketching, and community is discussed in the next few pages.

Sketching and Prototyping

Sketching is a way of thinking; it's playful and quick. The basic goal is to explore many ideas in a short amount of time. In our own work, we usually start by sketching on paper and then moving the results into code. Ideas for animation and interactions are usually sketched as storyboards with notations. After making some software sketches, the best ideas are selected and combined into prototypes (Figure 1-1). It's a cyclical process of making, testing, and improving that moves back and forth between paper and screen.

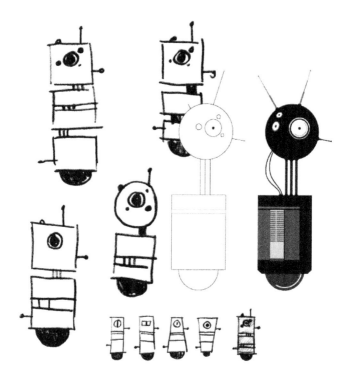

Figure 1-1. *As drawings move from sketchbook to screen, new possibilities emerge*

Flexibility

Like a software utility belt, Processing consists of many tools that work together in different combinations. As a result, it can be used for quick hacks or for in-depth research. Because a Processing program can be as short as one line or as long as thousands, there's room for growth and variation. More than 100 libraries extend Processing even further into domains including sound, computer vision, and digital fabrication (Figure 1-2).

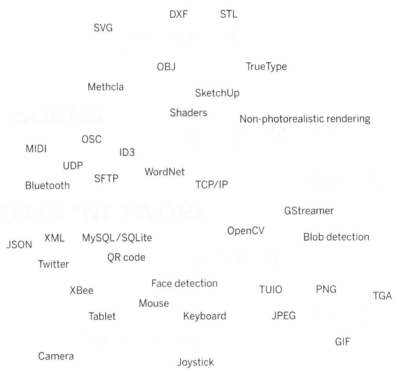

Figure 1-2. *Many types of information can flow in and out of Processing*

Giants

People have been making pictures with computers since the 1960s, and there's much to be learned from this history. For example, before computers could display to CRT or LCD screens, huge plotter machines such as the one shown in

Figure 1-3 were used to draw images. In life, we all stand on the shoulders of giants, and the titans for Processing include thinkers from design, computer graphics, art, architecture, statistics, and the spaces between. Have a look at Ivan Sutherland's *Sketchpad* (1963), Alan Kay's *Dynabook* (1968), and the many artists featured in Ruth Leavitt's *Artist and Computer*[1] (Harmony Books, 1976). The ACM SIGGRAPH and Ars Electronica archives provide fascinating glimpses into the history of graphics and software.

Figure 1-3. *Drawing demonstration by Manfred Mohr at Musée d'Art Moderne de la Ville de Paris using the Benson plotter and a digital computer on May 11, 1971 (photo by Rainer Mürle, courtesy bitforms gallery, New York)*

1 http://www.atariarchives.org/artist/

Family Tree

Like human languages, programming languages belong to families of related languages. Processing is a dialect of a programming language called Java; the language syntax is almost identical, but Processing adds custom features related to graphics and interaction (Figure 1-4). The graphic elements of Processing are related to PostScript (a foundation of PDF) and OpenGL (a 3D graphics specification). Because of these shared features, learning Processing is an entry-level step to programming in other languages and using different software tools.

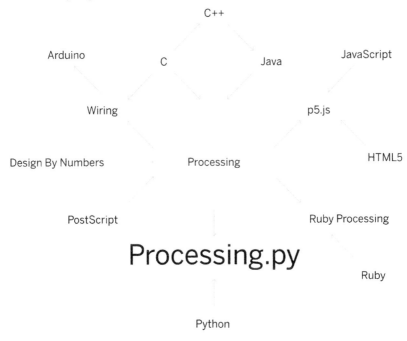

Figure 1-4. *Processing has a large family of related languages and programming environments*

Join In

Thousands of people use Processing every day. Like them, you can download Processing without cost. You even have the option to modify the Processing code to suit your needs. Processing is a *FLOSS* project (that is, *free/libre/open source soft-*

ware), and in the spirit of community, we encourage you to participate by sharing your projects and knowledge online at Processing.org and at the many social networking sites that host Processing content. These sites are linked from the Processing.org website (*http://processing.org*).

2/Starting to Code

To get the most out of this book, you need to do more than just read the words. You need to experiment and practice. You can't learn to code just by reading about it—you need to do it. To get started, download Processing and make your first sketch.

Start by visiting *http://processing.org/download* and selecting the OS X, Windows, or Linux version, depending on what machine you have. Installation on each machine is straightforward:

- On Windows, you'll have a *.zip* file. Double-click it, and drag the folder inside to a location on your hard disk. It could be *Program Files* or simply the desktop, but the important thing is for the *processing* folder to be pulled out of that *.zip* file. Then double-click *processing.exe* to start.

- The OS X version is a *.zip* file. Double-click it, and drag the Processing icon to the *Applications* folder. If you're using someone else's machine and can't modify the *Applications* folder, just drag the application to the desktop. Then double-click the Processing icon to start.

- The Linux version is a *.tar.gz* file, which should be familiar to most Linux users. Download the file to your home directory, then open a terminal window and type:

      tar xvfz processing-xxxx.tgz

(Replace *xxxx* with the rest of the file's name, which is the version number.) This will create a folder named *processing-3.0* or something similar.

Then change to that directory:

```
cd processing-xxxx
```

and run it:

```
./processing
```

With any luck, the main Processing window will now be visible (Figure 2-1). Everyone's setup is different, so if the program didn't start or you're otherwise stuck, visit the troubleshooting page (*https://github.com/jdf/Processing.py-Bugs/issues*) for possible solutions.

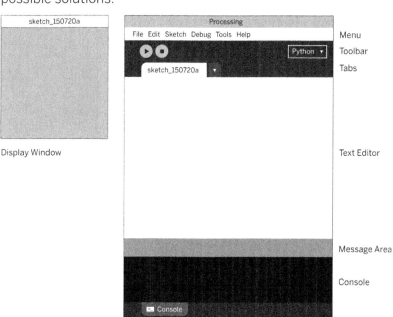

Figure 2-1. *The Processing Development Environment*

Python Mode

Processing doesn't include support for the Python programming language by default. In order to enable Python support, you'll need to install an add-on called *Python Mode*. You can do this by clicking on the drop-down menu on the right side of the toolbar and selecting Add Mode.... A window with the title Contribution Manager will appear. Click the tab labelled Modes and scroll down until you see Python Mode for Processing 3, then press Install.

After you've installed Python Mode, you can switch back and forth between the Python and Java versions of Processing using the drop-down menu in the toolbar. If you find yourself getting strange syntax errors or exceptions when running your program, make sure you have the right mode selected!

Your First Program

You're now running the Processing Development Environment (or PDE). There's not much to it. The large area is the Text Editor, and there are two buttons across the top—this is the toolbar. Below the editor is the Message Area, and below that is the Console. The Message Area is used for one-line messages, and the Console is used for more technical details.

Example 2-1: Draw an Ellipse

In the editor, type the following:

```
ellipse(50, 50, 80, 80)
```

This line of code means "draw an ellipse, with the center 50 pixels over from the left and 50 pixels down from the top, with a width and height of 80 pixels." Click the Run button (the triangle button in the Toolbar).

If you've typed everything correctly, you'll see a circle on the screen. If you didn't type it correctly, the Message Area will turn red and complain about an error. If this happens, make sure that you've copied the example code exactly; the numbers should be contained within parentheses and have commas between each of them.

One of the most difficult things about getting started with programming is that you have to be very specific about the syntax. The Processing software isn't always smart enough to know what you mean and can be quite fussy about the placement of punctuation. You'll get used to it with a little practice.

Next, we'll skip ahead to a sketch that's a little more exciting.

Example 2-2: Make Circles

Delete the text from the last example, and try this one:

```python
def setup():
    size(480, 120)

def draw():
    if mousePressed:
        fill(0)
    else:
        fill(255)
    ellipse(mouseX, mouseY, 80, 80)
```

Python is notoriously picky about formatting, so make sure you type the code exactly as shown, indentation and all.

This program creates a window that is 480 pixels wide and 120 pixels high, and then starts drawing white circles at the position of the mouse. When a mouse button is pressed, the circle color changes to black. We'll explain more about this program later. For now, run the code, move the mouse, and click to see what it does. While the sketch is running, the Run button will change to a square "stop" icon, which you can click to halt the sketch.

Show

If you don't want to use the buttons, you can always use the Sketch menu, which reveals the shortcut Ctrl-R (or Cmd-R on OS X) for Run. The Present option clears the rest of the screen when the program is run to present the sketch all by itself. You can also use Present from the toolbar by holding down the Shift key as you click the Run button. See Figure 2-2.

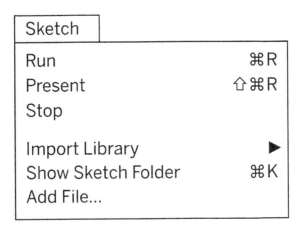

Figure 2-2. *A Processing sketch is displayed on screen with Run and Present. The Present option clears the entire screen before running the code for a cleaner presentation.*

Save and New

The next important command is Save. You can find it under the File menu. By default, your programs are saved to the *sketch-book*, which is a folder that collects your programs for easy access. Select the Sketchbook option in the File menu to bring up a list of all the sketches in your sketchbook.

It's always a good idea to save your sketches often. As you try different things, keep saving with different names so that you can always go back to an earlier version. This is especially help-ful if—no, *when*—something breaks. You can also see where the sketch is located on your computer with the Show Sketch Folder command under the Sketch menu.

You can create a new sketch by selecting the New option from the File Menu. This will create a new sketch in its own window.

Share

Processing sketches are made to be shared. The Export Appli-cation option in the File menu will bundle your code into a single folder. Export Application creates an application for your choice of OS X, Windows, and/or Linux. This is an easy way to make self-contained, double-clickable versions of your projects.

Select if you want the program to be full screen or in a window, and if there is a stop button and background color.

 The application folders are erased and re-created each time you use the Export Application command, so be sure to move the folder elsewhere if you do not want it to be erased with the next export.

Examples and Reference

Learning how to program involves exploring lots of code: running, altering, breaking, and enhancing it until you have reshaped it into something new. With this in mind, the Processing software download includes dozens of examples that demonstrate different features of the software. To open an example, select Examples from the File menu and double-click an example's name to open it. The examples are grouped into categories based on their function, such as Form, Motion, and Image. Find an interesting topic in the list and try an example. (The examples are specific to each Processing mode, so make sure you have Python Mode selected before you try to access them.)

The *Processing Reference for Python* (*http://py.processing.org/ reference/*) explains every code element with a description and examples. The *Processing Reference* programs are much shorter (usually four or five lines) and easier to follow than the longer code found in the *Examples* folder. We recommend keeping the *Processing Reference* open while you're reading this book and while you're programming. It can be navigated by topic or alphabetically, but sometimes it's fastest to do a text search within your browser window.

The *Processing Reference* was written with the beginner in mind; we hope that we've made it clear and understandable. We're grateful to the many people who've spotted errors over the years and reported them. If you think you can improve a reference entry or you find a mistake, please let us know by clicking on the link at the top of each reference page.

3/Draw

At first, drawing on a computer screen is like working on graph paper. It starts as a careful technical procedure, but as new concepts are introduced, drawing simple shapes with software expands into animation and interaction. Before we make this jump, we need to start at the beginning.

A computer screen is a grid of light elements called *pixels*. Each pixel has a position within the grid that is defined by coordinates. In Processing, the *x* coordinate is the distance from the left edge of the Display Window, and the *y* coordinate is the distance from the top edge. We write coordinates of a pixel like this: (x, y). So, if the screen is 200×200 pixels, the upper-left is (0, 0), the center is at (100, 100), and the lower-right is (199, 199). These numbers may seem confusing; why do we go from 0 to 199 instead of 1 to 200? The answer is that in code, we usually count from 0 because it's easier for calculations that we'll get into later.

The Display Window

The Display Window is created and images are drawn inside through code elements called *functions*. Functions are the basic building blocks of a Processing program. The behavior of a function is defined by its *parameters*. For example, almost every Processing program has a `size()` function to set the width and height of the Display Window. (If your program doesn't have a `size()` function, the dimension is set to 100×100 pixels.)

Example 3-1: Draw a Window

The `size()` function has two parameters: the first sets the width of the window and the second sets the height. To draw a window that is 800 pixels wide and 600 high, write:

```
size(800, 600)
```

Run this line of code to see the result. Put in different values to see what's possible. Try very small numbers and numbers larger than your screen.

Example 3-2: Draw a Point

To set the color of a single pixel within the Display Window, we use the `point()` function. It has two parameters that define a position: the *x* coordinate followed by the *y* coordinate. To draw a little window and a point at the center of the screen, coordinate (240, 60), type:

```
size(480, 120)
point(240, 60)
```

Try to write a program that puts a point at each corner of the Display Window and one in the center. Try placing points side by side to make horizontal, vertical, and diagonal lines.

Basic Shapes

Processing includes a group of functions to draw basic shapes (see Figure 3-1). Simple shapes like lines can be combined to create more complex forms like a leaf or a face.

To draw a single line, we need four parameters: two for the starting location and two for the end.

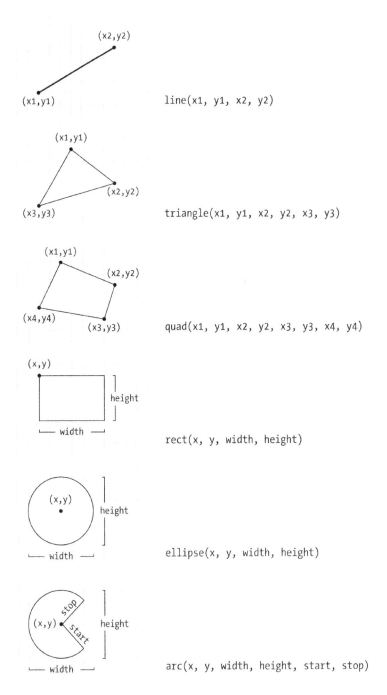

```
line(x1, y1, x2, y2)

triangle(x1, y1, x2, y2, x3, y3)

quad(x1, y1, x2, y2, x3, y3, x4, y4)

rect(x, y, width, height)

ellipse(x, y, width, height)

arc(x, y, width, height, start, stop)
```

Figure 3-1. *Shapes and their coordinates*

Example 3-3: Draw a Line

To draw a line between coordinate (20, 50) and (420, 110), try:

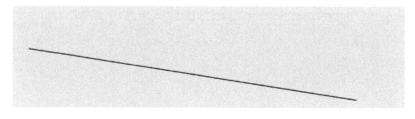

```
size(480, 120)
line(20, 50, 420, 110)
```

Example 3-4: Draw Basic Shapes

Following this pattern, a triangle needs six parameters and a quadrilateral needs eight (one pair for each point):

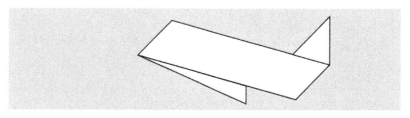

```
size(480, 120)
quad(158, 55, 199, 14, 392, 66, 351, 107)
triangle(347, 54, 392, 9, 392, 66)
triangle(158, 55, 290, 91, 290, 112)
```

Example 3-5: Draw a Rectangle

Rectangles and ellipses are both defined with four parameters: the first and second are for the *x* and *y* coordinates of the anchor point, the third for the width, and the fourth for the height. To make a rectangle at coordinate (180, 60) with a width of 220 pixels and height of 40, use the rect() function like this:

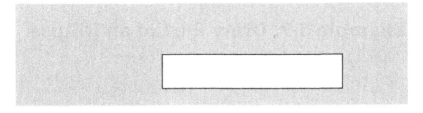

```
size(480, 120)
rect(180, 60, 220, 40)
```

Example 3-6: Draw an Ellipse

The x and y coordinates for a rectangle are the upper-left corner, but for an ellipse they are the center of the shape. In this example, notice that the y coordinate for the first ellipse is outside the window. Objects can be drawn partially (or entirely) out of the window without an error:

```
size(480, 120)
ellipse(278, -100, 400, 400)
ellipse(120, 100, 110, 110)
ellipse(412, 60, 18, 18)
```

Processing doesn't have separate functions to make squares and circles. To make these shapes, use the same value for the width and the height parameters for `ellipse()` and `rect()`.

Example 3-7: Draw Part of an Ellipse

The `arc()` function draws a piece of an ellipse:

```
size(480, 120)
arc(90, 60, 80, 80, 0, HALF_PI)
arc(190, 60, 80, 80, 0, PI+HALF_PI)
arc(290, 60, 80, 80, PI, TWO_PI+HALF_PI)
arc(390, 60, 80, 80, QUARTER_PI, PI+QUARTER_PI)
```

The first and second parameters set the location, the third and fourth set the width and height. The fifth parameter sets the angle to start the arc, and the sixth sets the angle to stop. The angles are set in radians, rather than degrees. Radians are angle measurements based on the value of pi (3.14159). Figure 3-2 shows the relationship between radians and degrees. As featured in this example, four radian values are used so frequently that special names for them were added as a part of Processing. The values PI, QUARTER_PI, HALF_PI, and TWO_PI can be used to replace the radian values for 180°, 45°, 90°, and 360°.

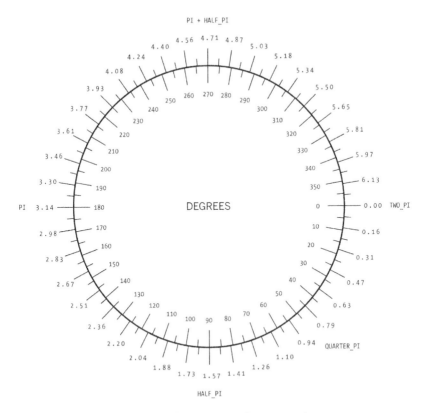

Figure 3-2. *Radians and degrees are two ways to measure an angle. Degrees move around the circle from 0 to 360, while radians measure the angles in relation to pi, from 0 to approximately 6.28.*

Example 3-8: Draw with Degrees

If you prefer to use degree measurements, you can convert to radians with the `radians()` function. This function takes an angle in degrees and changes it to the corresponding radian value. The following example is the same as Example 3-7 on page 18, but it uses the `radians()` function to define the start and stop values in degrees:

```
size(480, 120)
arc(90, 60, 80, 80, 0, radians(90))
```

```
arc(190, 60, 80, 80, 0, radians(270))
arc(290, 60, 80, 80, radians(180), radians(450))
arc(390, 60, 80, 80, radians(45), radians(225))
```

Drawing Order

When a program runs, the computer starts at the top and reads each line of code until it reaches the last line, and then stops. If you want a shape to be drawn on top of all other shapes, it needs to follow the others in the code.

Example 3-9: Control Your Drawing Order

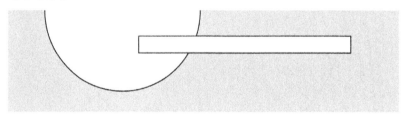

```
size(480, 120)
ellipse(140, 0, 190, 190)
# The rectangle draws on top of the ellipse because it
# comes after in the code
rect(160, 30, 260, 20)
```

Example 3-10: Put It in Reverse

Modify by reversing the order of `rect()` and `ellipse()` to see the circle on top of the rectangle:

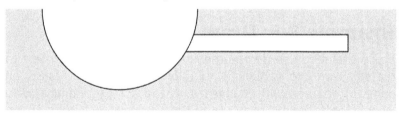

```
size(480, 120)
rect(160, 30, 260, 20)
# The ellipse draws on top of the rectangle because it
```

```
# comes after in the code
ellipse(140, 0, 190, 190)
```

You can think of it like painting with a brush or making a collage. The last element that you add is what's visible on top.

Shape Properties

The most basic and useful shape properties are stroke weight, the way the ends (caps) of lines are drawn, and how the corners of shapes are displayed.

Example 3-11: Set Stroke Weight

The default stroke weight is a single pixel, but this can be changed with the strokeWeight() function. The single parameter to strokeWeight() sets the width of drawn lines:

```
size(480, 120)
ellipse(75, 60, 90, 90)
strokeWeight(8)  # Stroke weight to 8 pixels
ellipse(175, 60, 90, 90)
ellipse(279, 60, 90, 90)
strokeWeight(20)  # Stroke weight to 20 pixels
ellipse(389, 60, 90, 90)
```

Example 3-12: Set Stroke Caps

The strokeCap() function changes how lines are drawn at their endpoints. By default, they have rounded ends:

```
size(480, 120)
strokeWeight(24)
line(60, 25, 130, 95)
strokeCap(SQUARE)    # Square the line endings
line(160, 25, 230, 95)
strokeCap(PROJECT)   # Project the line endings
line(260, 25, 330, 95)
strokeCap(ROUND)     # Round the line endings
line(360, 25, 430, 95)
```

Example 3-13: Set Stroke Joins

The strokeJoin() function changes the way lines are joined
(how the corners look). By default, they have pointed (mitered)
corners:

```
size(480, 120)
strokeWeight(12)
rect(60, 25, 70, 70)
strokeJoin(ROUND)    # Round the stroke corners
rect(160, 25, 70, 70)
strokeJoin(BEVEL)    # Bevel the stroke corners
rect(260, 25, 70, 70)
strokeJoin(MITER)    # Miter the stroke corners
rect(360, 25, 70, 70)
```

When any of these attributes are set, all shapes drawn afterward
are affected. For instance, in Example 3-11 on page 21, notice
how the second and third circles both have the same stroke
weight even though the weight is set only once before both are
drawn.

Drawing Modes

A group of functions with "mode" in their name change how
Processing draws geometry to the screen. In this chapter, we'll
look at ellipseMode() and rectMode(), which help us to draw

ellipses and rectangles, respectively. Later in the book, we'll cover imageMode() and shapeMode().

Example 3-14: On the Corner

By default, the ellipse() function uses its first two parameters as the *x* and *y* coordinate of the center and the third and fourth parameters as the width and height. After ellipseMode(CORNER) is run in a sketch, the first two parameters to ellipse() then define the position of the upper-left corner of the rectangle the ellipse is inscribed within. This makes the ellipse() function behave more like rect(), as seen in this example:

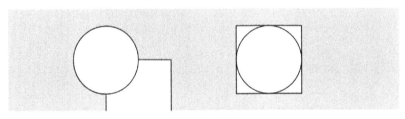

```
size(480, 120)
rect(120, 60, 80, 80)
ellipse(120, 60, 80, 80)
ellipseMode(CORNER)
rect(280, 20, 80, 80)
ellipse(280, 20, 80, 80)
```

You'll find these "mode" functions in examples throughout the book. There are more options for how to use them in the *Processing Reference*.

Color

All the shapes so far have been filled white with black outlines, and the background of the Display Window has been light gray. To change them, use the background(), fill(), and stroke() functions. The values of the parameters are in the range of 0 to 255, where 255 is white, 128 is medium gray, and 0 is black. Figure 3-3 shows how the values from 0 to 255 map to different colors.

	R	G	B		R	G	B
	255	204	0		0	102	204
	249	201	4		5	105	205
	243	199	9		11	108	206
	238	197	13		17	112	207
	232	194	18		22	115	208
	226	192	22		28	119	209
	221	190	27		34	122	210
	215	188	31		39	125	211
	209	185	36		45	129	213
	204	183	40		51	132	214
	198	181	45		56	136	215
	192	179	49		62	139	216
	187	176	54		68	142	217
	181	174	58		73	146	218
	175	172	63		79	149	219
	170	170	68		85	153	221
	164	167	72		90	156	222
	158	165	77		96	159	223
	153	163	81		102	163	224
	147	160	86		107	166	225
	141	158	90		113	170	226
	136	156	95		119	173	227
	130	154	99		124	176	228
	124	151	104		130	180	230
	119	149	108		136	183	231
	113	147	113		141	187	232
	107	145	117		147	190	233
	102	142	122		153	193	234
	96	140	126		158	197	235
	90	138	131		164	200	236
	85	136	136		170	204	238
	79	133	140		175	207	239
	73	131	145		181	210	240
	68	129	149		187	214	241
	62	126	154		192	217	242
	56	124	158		198	221	243
	51	122	163		204	224	244
	45	120	167		209	227	245
	39	117	172		215	231	247
	34	115	176		221	234	248
	28	113	181		226	238	249
	22	111	185		232	241	250
	17	108	190		238	244	251
	11	106	194		243	248	252
	5	104	199		249	251	253
	0	102	204		255	255	255

Figure 3-3. *Colors are created by defining RGB (red, green, blue) values*

Example 3-15: Paint with Grays

This example shows three different gray values on a black background:

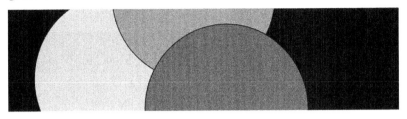

```
size(480, 120)
background(0) # Black
fill(204) # Light gray
ellipse(132, 82, 200, 200) # Light gray circle
fill(153) # Medium gray
ellipse(228, -16, 200, 200) # Medium gray circle
fill(102) # Dark gray
ellipse(268, 118, 200, 200) # Dark gray circle
```

Example 3-16: Control Fill and Stroke

You can disable the stroke so that there's no outline by using
noStroke(), and you can disable the fill of a shape with noFill():

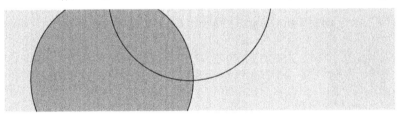

```
size(480, 120)
fill(153) # Medium gray
ellipse(132, 82, 200, 200) # Gray circle
noFill() # Turn off fill
ellipse(228, -16, 200, 200) # Outline circle
noStroke() # Turn off stroke
ellipse(268, 118, 200, 200) # Doesn't draw!
```

Be careful not to disable the fill and stroke at the same time, as
we've done in the previous example, because nothing will draw
to the screen.

Example 3-17: Draw with Color

To move beyond grayscale values, you use three parameters to specify the red, green, and blue components of a color.

Run the code in Processing to reveal the colors:

```
size(480, 120)
noStroke()
background(0, 26, 51) # Dark blue color
fill(255, 0, 0) # Red color
ellipse(132, 82, 200, 200) # Red circle
fill(0, 255, 0) # Green color
ellipse(228, -16, 200, 200) # Green circle
fill(0, 0, 255) # Blue color
ellipse(268, 118, 200, 200) # Blue circle
```

This is referred to as RGB color, which comes from how computers define colors on the screen. The three numbers stand for the values of red, green, and blue, and they range from 0 to 255, the same way that the gray values do. Using RGB color isn't very intuitive, so to choose colors, use Tools→Color Selector, which shows a color palette similar to those found in other software (see Figure 3-4). Select a color, and then use the R, G, and B values as the parameters for your **background()**, **fill()**, or **stroke()** function.

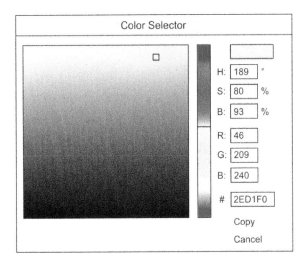

Color Selector

H: 189 °
S: 80 %
B: 93 %

R: 46
G: 209
B: 240

2ED1F0

Copy

Cancel

Figure 3-4. *Processing Color Selector*

Example 3-18: Set Transparency

By adding an optional fourth parameter to `fill()` or `stroke()`, you can control the transparency. This fourth parameter is known as the *alpha* value, and also uses the range 0 to 255 to set the amount of transparency. The value 0 defines the color as entirely transparent (it won't display), the value 255 is entirely opaque, and the values between these extremes cause the colors to mix on screen:

```
size(480, 120)
noStroke()
background(204, 226, 225) # Light blue color
fill(255, 0, 0, 160) # Red color
ellipse(132, 82, 200, 200) # Red circle
fill(0, 255, 0, 160) # Green color
ellipse(228, -16, 200, 200) # Green circle
```

```
fill(0, 0, 255, 160) # Blue color
ellipse(268, 118, 200, 200) # Blue circle
```

Custom Shapes

You're not limited to using these basic geometric shapes—you can also define new shapes by connecting a series of points.

Example 3-19: Draw an Arrow

The beginShape() function signals the start of a new shape. The vertex() function is used to define each pair of *x* and *y* coordinates for the shape. Finally, endShape() is called to signal that the shape is finished:

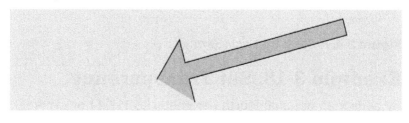

```
size(480, 120)
beginShape()
fill(153, 176, 180)
vertex(180, 82)
vertex(207, 36)
vertex(214, 63)
vertex(407, 11)
vertex(412, 30)
vertex(219, 82)
vertex(226, 109)
endShape()
```

Example 3-20: Close the Gap

When you run Example 3-19 on page 28, you'll see the first and last point are not connected. To do this, add the word CLOSE as a parameter to endShape(), like this:

```
size(480, 120)
beginShape()
fill(153, 176, 180)
vertex(180, 82)
vertex(207, 36)
vertex(214, 63)
vertex(407, 11)
vertex(412, 30)
vertex(219, 82)
vertex(226, 109)
endShape(CLOSE)
```

Example 3-21: Create Some Creatures

The power of defining shapes with vertex() is the ability to make shapes with complex outlines. Processing can draw thousands and thousands of lines at a time to fill the screen with fantastic shapes that spring from your imagination. A modest but more complex example follows:

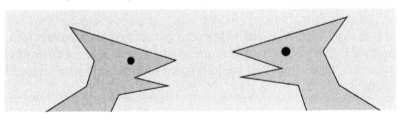

```
size(480, 120)

# Left creature
fill(153, 176, 180);
beginShape()
vertex(50, 120)
vertex(100, 90)
vertex(110, 60)
vertex(80, 20)
vertex(210, 60)
```

```
vertex(160, 80)
vertex(200, 90)
vertex(140, 100)
vertex(130, 120)
endShape()
fill(0)
ellipse(155, 60, 8, 8)

# Right creature
fill(176, 186, 163);
beginShape()
vertex(370, 120)
vertex(360, 90)
vertex(290, 80)
vertex(340, 70)
vertex(280, 50)
vertex(420, 10)
vertex(390, 50)
vertex(410, 90)
vertex(460, 120)
endShape()
fill(0)
ellipse(345, 50, 10, 10)
```

Comments

The examples in this chapter use a number symbol (#) at the end of a line to add comments to the code. Comments are parts of the program that are ignored when the program is run. They are useful for making notes for yourself that explain what's happening in the code. If others are reading your code, comments are especially important to help them understand your thought process.

Comments are also useful for a number of other purposes, such as when trying to choose the right color. So, for instance, I might be trying to find just the right red for an ellipse:

```
size(200, 200)
fill(165, 57, 57)
ellipse(100, 100, 80, 80)
```

Now suppose I want to try a different red, but don't want to lose the old one. I can copy and paste the line, make a change, and then "comment out" the old one:

```
size(200, 200)
#fill(165, 57, 57)
fill(144, 39, 39)
ellipse(100, 100, 80, 80)
```

Placing # at the beginning of the line temporarily disables it. Or I can remove the # and place it in front of the other line if I want to try it again:

```
size(200, 200)
fill(165, 57, 57)
#fill(144, 39, 39)
ellipse(100, 100, 80, 80)
```

As you work with Processing sketches, you'll find yourself creating dozens of iterations of ideas; using comments to make notes or to disable code can help you keep track of multiple options.

 As a shortcut, you can also use Ctrl-/ (Cmd-/ on OS X) to add or remove comments from the current line or a selected block of text.

Robot 1: Draw

This is P5, the Processing Robot. There are 10 different programs to draw and animate him in the book—each one explores a different programming idea. P5's design was inspired by Sputnik I (1957), Shakey from the Stanford Research Institute (1966–1972), the fighter drone in David Lynch's *Dune* (1984), and HAL 9000 from *2001: A Space Odyssey* (1968), among other robot favorites.

The first robot program uses the drawing functions introduced in this chapter. The parameters to the `fill()` and `stroke()` functions set the gray values. The `line()`, `ellipse()`, and `rect()` functions define the shapes that create the robot's neck, antennae, body, and head. To get more familiar with the functions, run the program and change the values to redesign the robot:

```
size(720, 480)
strokeWeight(2)
background(0, 153, 204) # Blue background
ellipseMode(RADIUS)

# Neck
stroke(255) # Set stroke to white
line(266, 257, 266, 162) # Left
line(276, 257, 276, 162) # Middle
line(286, 257, 286, 162) # Right

# Antennae
line(276, 155, 246, 112) # Small
line(276, 155, 306, 56) # Tall
line(276, 155, 342, 170) # Medium

# Body
noStroke() # Disable stroke
fill(255, 204, 0) # Set fill to orange
ellipse(264, 377, 33, 33) # Antigravity orb
fill(0) # Set fill to black
rect(219, 257, 90, 120) # Main body
fill(102) # Set fill to gray
rect(219, 274, 90, 6) # Gray stripe

# Head
fill(0) # Set fill to black
ellipse(276, 155, 45, 45) # Head
fill(255) # Set fill to white
ellipse(288, 150, 14, 14) # Large eye
```

```
fill(0) # Set fill to black
ellipse(288, 150, 3, 3) # Pupil
fill(153, 204, 255) # Set fill to light blue
ellipse(263, 148, 5, 5) # Small eye 1
ellipse(296, 130, 4, 4) # Small eye 2
ellipse(305, 162, 3, 3) # Small eye 3
```

4/Variables

A *variable* stores a value in memory so that it can be used later in a program. The variable can be used many times within a single program, and the value is easily changed while the program is running.

First Variables

One of the reasons we use variables is to avoid repeating ourselves in the code. If you are typing the same number more than once, consider making it into a variable to make your code more general and easier to update.

Example 4-1: Reuse the Same Values

For instance, when you make the y coordinate and diameter for the two circles in this example into variables, the same values are used for each ellipse:

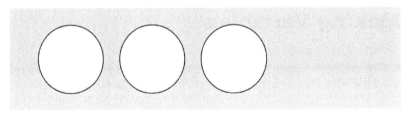

```
size(480, 120)
y = 60
d = 80
ellipse(75, y, d, d)     # Left
ellipse(175, y, d, d)    # Middle
ellipse(275, y, d, d)    # Right
```

Example 4-2: Change Values

Simply changing the y and d variables alters all three ellipses:

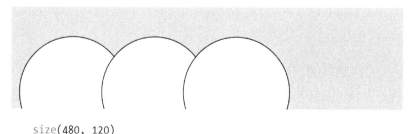

```
size(480, 120)
y = 100
d = 130
ellipse(75, y, d, d)      # Left
ellipse(175, y, d, d)     # Middle
ellipse(275, y, d, d)     # Right
```

Without the variables, you'd need to change the *y* coordinate used in the code three times and the diameter six times. When comparing Example 4-1 on page 35 and Example 4-2 on page 36, notice how the bottom three lines of code are the same, and only the middle two lines with the variables are different. Variables allow you to separate the lines of the code that change from the lines that don't, which makes programs easier to modify. For instance, if you place variables that control colors and sizes of shapes in one place, then you can quickly explore different visual options by focusing on only a few lines of code.

Making Variables

When you make your own variables, you determine the *name* and the *value*. The name is what you decide to call the variable. Choose a name that is informative about what the variable stores, but be consistent and not too verbose. For instance, the variable name "radius" will be clearer than "r" when you look at the code later.

The range of values that can be stored within a variable is defined by its *data type*. For instance, the *integer* data type can store numbers without decimal places (whole numbers). There are data types to store each kind of data: integers, floating-point (decimal) numbers, words, images, fonts, and so on. Python automatically determines the data type of a variable based on the value you assign to it.

Processing Variables

Processing has a series of special variables to store information about the program while it runs. For instance, the width and height of the window are stored in variables called `width` and `height`. These values are set by the `size()` function. They can be used to draw elements relative to the size of the window, even if the `size()` line changes.

Example 4-3: Adjust the Size, See What Follows

In this example, change the parameters to `size()` to see how it works:

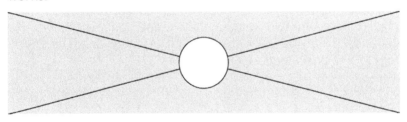

```
size(480, 120)
line(0, 0, width, height) # Line from (0,0) to (480, 120)
line(width, 0, 0, height) # Line from (480, 0) to (0, 120)
ellipse(width/2, height/2, 60, 60)
```

Other special variables keep track of the status of the mouse and keyboard values and much more. These are discussed in Chapter 5.

A Little Math

People often assume that math and programming are the same thing. Although knowledge of math can be useful for certain types of coding, basic arithmetic covers the most important parts.

Example 4-4: Basic Arithmetic

```
size(480, 120)
x = 25
h = 20
y = 25
rect(x, y, 300, h)          # Top
x = x + 100
rect(x, y + h, 300, h)      # Middle
x = x - 250
rect(x, y + h*2, 300, h)   # Bottom
```

In code, symbols like +, -, and * are called *operators*. When placed between two values, they create an *expression*. For instance, 5 + 9 and 1024 - 512 are both expressions. The operators for the basic math operations are:

+	Addition
−	Subtraction
*	Multiplication
/	Division
=	Assignment

Python has a set of rules to define which operators take precedence over others, meaning which calculations are made first, second, third, and so on. These rules define the order in which the code is run. A little knowledge about this goes a long way toward understanding how a short line of code like this works:

```
x = 4 + 4 * 5  # Assign 24 to x
```

The expression 4 * 5 is evaluated first because multiplication has the highest priority. Second, 4 is added to the product of 4 * 5 to yield 24. This is clarified with parentheses, but the result is the same:

```
x = 4 + (4 * 5)   # Assign 24 to x
```

If you want to force the addition to happen first, just move the parentheses. Because parentheses have a higher precedence than multiplication, the order is changed and the calculation is affected:

```
x = (4 + 4) * 5   # Assign 40 to x
```

An acronym for this order is often taught in math class: PEMDAS, which stands for Parentheses, Exponents, Multiplication, Division, Addition, Subtraction, where parentheses have the highest priority and subtraction the lowest. The complete order of operations is found in Appendix C.

Some calculations are used so frequently in programming that shortcuts have been developed; it's always nice to save a few keystrokes. For instance, you can add to a variable, or subtract from it, with a single operator:

```
x += 10   # This is the same as x = x + 10
y -= 15   # This is the same as y = y - 15
```

More shortcuts can be found in the *Processing Reference*.

Repetition

As you write more programs, you'll notice that patterns occur when lines of code are repeated, but with slight variations. A code structure called a *for loop* makes it possible to run a line of code more than once to condense this type of repetition into fewer lines. This makes your programs more modular and easier to change.

Example 4-5: Do the Same Thing Over and Over

This example has the type of pattern that can be simplified with a for loop:

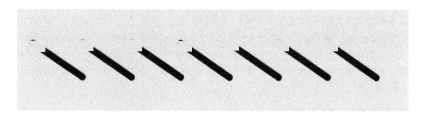

```
size(480, 120)
strokeWeight(8)
line(20, 40, 80, 80)
line(80, 40, 140, 80)
line(140, 40, 200, 80)
line(200, 40, 260, 80)
line(260, 40, 320, 80)
line(320, 40, 380, 80)
line(380, 40, 440, 80)
```

Example 4-6: Use a for Loop

The same thing can be done with a for loop, and with less code:

```
size(480, 120)
strokeWeight(8)
for i in range(20, 400, 60):
    line(i, 40, i + 60, 80)
```

The for loop is different in many ways from the code we've written so far. Notice the colon (:) at the end of the line that begins with for, and how the line directly beneath it is *indented* (i.e., moved over from the lefthand margin with some whitespace). The indented code between the braces is called a *block*. This is the code that will be repeated on each iteration of the for loop.

The for loop has several moving parts. Between the word for and the word in, there is a variable name, which we'll call the *target variable*. Inside the parentheses, following the word range, there are three values, separated by commas: *start*, *stop*, and *step*. These three values determine how many times the code inside the block is run, and what value the target variable will have on each iteration of the loop:

```
for target_variable in range(start, stop, step):
    statements
```

The *start* value determines what value the target variable will have on the first iteration of the loop. On the second iteration of the loop, the *step* will be added to the *start* value, and the value of the *target_variable* will reflect this. This continues until the resulting value is greater than or equal to the *step* value, at which point the loop terminates.

You can use whatever name you'd like for the target variable, as long as it's a valid variable name in Python. The variable name i is frequently used, but there's really nothing special about it.

Example 4-7: Flex Your for Loop's Muscles

The ultimate power of working with a for loop is the ability to make quick changes to the code. Because the code inside the block is typically run multiple times, a change to the block is magnified when the code is run. By modifying Example 4-6 on page 40 only slightly, we can create a range of different patterns:

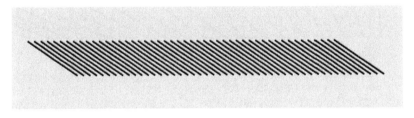

```
size(480, 120)
strokeWeight(2)
for i in range(20, 400, 8):
  line(i, 40, i + 60, 80)
```

Example 4-8: Fanning Out the Lines

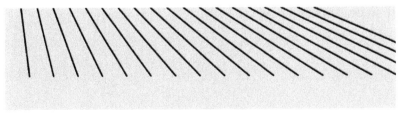

```
size(480, 120)
strokeWeight(2)
for i in range(20, 400, 20):
  line(i, 0, i + i/2, 80)
```

Example 4-9: Kinking the Lines

In this example, we're drawing *two* lines inside of the for loop (not just one). Both statements are indented, which tells Python that both statements should be executed for each iteration of the loop. It's important in Python to use *exactly* the same keystrokes to indent multiple statements in the same for loop. (Otherwise, you might get a syntax error.) For example, if the first statement in the for loop is indented with two space characters, the second statement must be indented with two space characters as well.

```
size(480, 120)
strokeWeight(2)
for i in range(20, 400, 20):
  line(i, 0, i + i/2, 80)
  line(i + i/2, 80, i*1.2, 120)
```

Example 4-10: Embed One for Loop in Another

When one for loop is embedded inside another, the number of repetitions is multiplied. First, let's look at a short example, and then we'll break it down in Example 4-11 on page 43:

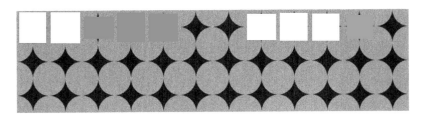

```
size(480, 120)
background(0)
noStroke()
for y in range(0, height+45, 40):
  for x in range(0, width+45, 40):
    fill(255, 140)
    ellipse(x, y, 40, 40)
```

Example 4-11: Rows and Columns

In this example, the for loops are adjacent, rather than one embedded inside the other. The result shows that one for loop is drawing a column of four circles and the other is drawing a row of 13 circles:

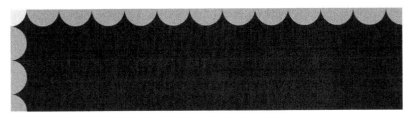

```
size(480, 120)
background(0)
noStroke()
for y in range(0, height+45, 40):
  fill(255, 140)
  ellipse(0, y, 40, 40)
for x in range(0, width+45, 40):
  fill(255, 140)
  ellipse(x, 0, 40, 40)
```

When one of these for loops is placed inside the other, as in Example 4-10 on page 42, the four repetitions of the first loop are compounded with the 13 of the second in order to run the code inside the embedded block 52 times (4×13 = 52).

Example 4-10 on page 42 is a good base for exploring many types of repeating visual patterns. The following examples show a couple of ways that it can be extended, but this is only a tiny sample of what's possible. In Example 4-12 on page 44, the code draws a line from each point in the grid to the center of the screen. In Example 4-13 on page 44, the ellipses shrink with each new row and are moved to the right by adding the *y* coordinate to the *x* coordinate.

Example 4-12: Pins and Lines

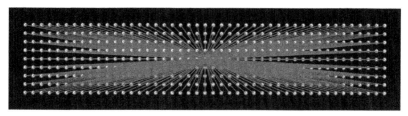

```
size(480, 120)
background(0)
fill(255)
stroke(102)
for y in range(20, height-15, 10):
  for x in range(20, width-15, 10):
    ellipse(x, y, 4, 4)
    # Draw a line to the center of the display
    line(x, y, 240, 60)
```

Example 4-13: Halftone Dots

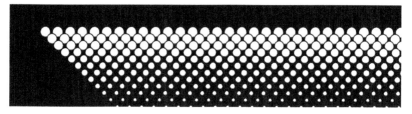

```
size(480, 120)
background(0)
for y in range(32, height, 8):
  for x in range(12, width, 15):
    ellipse(x + y, y, 16 - y/10.0, 16 - y/10.0)
```

Robot 2: Variables

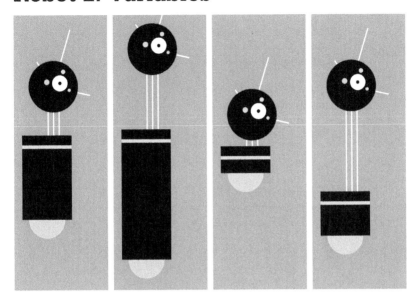

The variables introduced in this program make the code look more difficult than Robot 1 (see "Robot 1: Draw" on page 31), but now it's much easier to modify, because numbers that depend on one another are in a single location. For instance, the neck can be drawn based on the bodyHeight variable. The group of variables at the top of the code control the aspects of the robot that we want to change: location, body height, and neck height. You can see some of the range of possible variations in the figure. From left to right, here are the values that correspond to them:

y = 390	y = 460	y = 310	y = 420
bodyHeight = 180	bodyHeight = 260	bodyHeight = 80	bodyHeight = 110
neckHeight = 40	neckHeight = 95	neckHeight = 10	neckHeight = 140

When altering your own code to use variables instead of numbers, plan the changes carefully, then make the modifications in short steps. For instance, when this program was written, each variable was created one at a time to minimize the complexity of the transition. After a variable was added and the code was run to ensure it was working, the next variable was added:

```
x = 60              # x coordinate
y = 420             # y coordinate
bodyHeight = 110    # Body height
neckHeight = 140    # Neck height
radius = 45         # Head radius
ny = y - bodyHeight - neckHeight - radius  # Neck Y

size(170, 480)
strokeWeight(2)
background(0, 153, 204)
ellipseMode(RADIUS)

# Neck
stroke(102)
line(x+2, y-bodyHeight, x+2, ny)
line(x+12, y-bodyHeight, x+12, ny)
line(x+22, y-bodyHeight, x+22, ny)

# Antennae
line(x+12, ny, x-18, ny-43)
line(x+12, ny, x+42, ny-99)
line(x+12, ny, x+78, ny+15)

# Body
noStroke()
fill(255, 204, 0)
ellipse(x, y-33, 33, 33)
fill(0)
rect(x-45, y-bodyHeight, 90, bodyHeight-33)
fill(102)
rect(x-45, y-bodyHeight+17, 90, 6)

# Head
fill(0)
ellipse(x+12, ny, radius, radius)
fill(255)
ellipse(x+24, ny-6, 14, 14)
fill(0)
ellipse(x+24, ny-6, 3, 3)
fill(153)
ellipse(x, ny-8, 5, 5)
ellipse(x+30, ny-26, 4, 4)
ellipse(x+41, ny+6, 3, 3)
```

5/Response

Code that responds to input from the mouse, keyboard, and other devices has to run continuously. To make this happen, place the lines that update inside a Processing function called **draw()**.

Once and Forever

The code within the **draw()** block runs from top to bottom, then repeats until you quit the program by clicking the Stop button or closing the window. Each trip through **draw()** is called a *frame*. (The default frame rate is 60 frames per second, but this can be changed.)

Example 5-1: The draw() Function

To see how **draw()** works, run this example:

```
def draw():
  # Displays the frame count to the Console
  print "I'm drawing"
  print frameCount
```

You'll see the following:

```
I'm drawing
1
I'm drawing
2
I'm drawing
3
...
```

In this example program, the **print** statements write the text "I'm drawing" followed by the current frame count as counted by the special **frameCount** variable (1, 2, 3, ...). The text appears in the Console, the black area at the bottom of the Processing editor window.

Example 5-2: The setup() Function

To complement the looping draw() function, Processing has a function called setup() that runs just once when the program starts:

```
def setup():
    print "I'm starting"

def draw():
    print "I'm running"
```

When this code is run, the following is written to the Console:

```
I'm starting
I'm running
I'm running
I'm running
...
```

The text "I'm running" continues to write to the Console until the program is stopped.

In a typical program, the code inside setup() is used to define the starting values. The first line is always the size() function, often followed by code to set the starting fill and stroke colors, or perhaps to load images and fonts. (If you don't include the size() function, the Display Window will be 100×100 pixels.)

Now you know how to use setup() and draw(), but this isn't the whole story. There's one more location to put code—you can also place variables outside of setup() and draw(). If you create a variable inside of setup(), you can't use it inside of draw(), so you need to place those variables somewhere else. Such variables are called *global* variables, because they can be used anywhere ("globally") in the program. This is clearer when we list the order in which the code is run:

1. Variables declared outside of setup() and draw() are created.

2. Code inside setup() is run once.

3. Code inside `draw()` is run continuously.

Example 5-3: Global Variables

The following example puts it all together:

```
x = 280
y = -100
diameter = 380

def setup():
  size(480, 120)
  fill(102)

def draw():
  background(204)
  ellipse(x, y, diameter, diameter)
```

Follow

Now that we have code running continuously, we can track the mouse position and use those numbers to move elements on screen.

Example 5-4: Track the Mouse

The `mouseX` variable stores the *x* coordinate, and the `mouseY` variable stores the *y* coordinate:

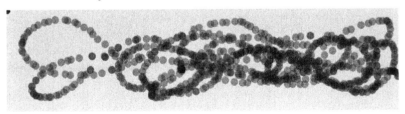

```
def setup():
  size(480, 120)
  fill(0, 102)
  noStroke()

def draw():
  ellipse(mouseX, mouseY, 9, 9)
```

In this example, each time the code in the `draw()` block is run, a new circle is drawn to the window. This image was made by moving the mouse around to control the circle's location. Because the fill is set to be partially transparent, denser black areas show where the mouse spent more time and where it moved slowly. The circles that are spaced farther apart show when the mouse was moving faster.

Example 5-5: The Dot Follows You

In this example, a new circle is added to the window each time the code in `draw()` is run. To refresh the screen and only display the newest circle, place a `background()` function at the begin ning of `draw()` before the shape is drawn:

```
def setup():
    size(480, 120)
    fill(0, 102)
    noStroke()

def draw():
    background(204)
    ellipse(mouseX, mouseY, 9, 9)
```

The `background()` function clears the entire window, so be sure to always place it before other functions inside `draw()`; otherwise, the shapes drawn before it will be erased.

Example 5-6: Draw Continuously

The `pmouseX` and `pmouseY` variables store the position of the mouse at the previous frame. Like `mouseX` and `mouseY`, these special variables are updated each time `draw()` runs. When combined, they can be used to draw continuous lines by connecting the current and most recent location:

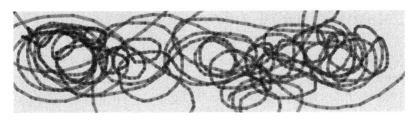

```
def setup():
    size(480, 120)
    strokeWeight(4)
    stroke(0, 102)

def draw():
    line(mouseX, mouseY, pmouseX, pmouseY)
```

Example 5-7: Set Thickness on the Fly

The pmouseX and pmouseY variables can also be used to calculate the speed of the mouse. This is done by measuring the distance between the current and most recent mouse location. If the mouse is moving slowly, the distance is small, but if the mouse starts moving faster, the distance grows. A function called dist() simplifies this calculation, as shown in the following example. Here, the speed of the mouse is used to set the thickness of the drawn line:

```
def setup():
    size(480, 120)
    stroke(0, 102)

def draw():
    weight = dist(mouseX, mouseY, pmouseX, pmouseY)
    strokeWeight(weight)
    line(mouseX, mouseY, pmouseX, pmouseY)
```

Example 5-8: Easing Does It

In Example 5-7 on page 51, the values from the mouse are converted directly into positions on the screen. But sometimes you want the values to follow the mouse loosely—to lag behind to create a more fluid motion. This technique is called *easing*. With easing, there are two values: the current value and the value to move toward (see Figure 5-1). At each step in the program, the current value moves a little closer to the target value:

```
x = 0.0
easing = 0.01

def setup():
    size(220, 120)

def draw():
    global x
    targetX = mouseX
    x += (targetX - x) * easing
    ellipse(x, 40, 12, 12)
    print targetX, x
```

The value of the x variable is always getting closer to targetX. The speed at which it catches up with targetX is set with the easing variable, a number between 0 and 1—a small value causes more of a delay than a larger value. With an easing value of 1, there is no delay. When you run Example 5-8 on page 52, the actual values are shown in the Console through the print statement. When moving the mouse, notice how the numbers are far apart, but when the mouse stops moving, the x value gets closer to targetX.

easing = 0.1

START   TARGET

easing = 0.2

START   TARGET

easing = 0.3

START   TARGET

easing = 0.4

START   TARGET

Figure 5-1. *Easing changes the number of steps it takes to move from one place to another*

All of the work in this example happens on the line that begins x +=. There, the difference between the target and current value is calculated, then multiplied by the easing variable and added to x to bring it closer to the target.

You may have noticed the global keyword on the first line of the draw() function. We'll discuss the purpose of this keyword in "Modifying Global Variables" on page 54.

Example 5-9: Smooth Lines with Easing

In this example, the easing technique is applied to Example 5-7 on page 51. In comparison, the lines are more fluid:

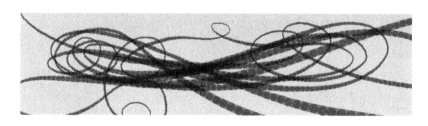

```
x = 0.0
y = 0.0
px = 0.0
py = 0.0
easing = 0.05;

def setup():
    size(480, 120)
    stroke(0, 102)

def draw():
    global x, y, px, py
    targetX = mouseX;
    x += (targetX - x) * easing
    targetY = mouseY
    y += (targetY - y) * easing
    weight = dist(x, y, px, py)
    strokeWeight(weight)
    line(x, y, px, py)
    py = y
    px = x
```

Modifying Global Variables

As explained earlier, a variable is *global* if the first time you assign a value to the variable occurs outside of a function (e.g., outside of *draw* and *setup*). You can use a global variable anywhere in your program without worries, as long as you're only using the variable's existing value in statements and expressions. However, if you want to *change* the value of a global variable from within a function (like **draw()** or **setup()**), you have to perform an extra step: include the **global** keyword as the first line in your function, with the name of the variable you want to change after the keyword. Here's what it looks like:

```
x = 0
def draw():
  global x
  x = x + 1
  ellipse(x, height/2, 10, 10)
```

If you want to modify multiple variables in the same function, put a comma-separated list of the variable names after the `global` keyword:

```
x = 0
y = 0
def draw():
  global x, y
  x = x + 1
  y = y + 1
  ellipse(x, y, 10, 10)
```

The `global` keyword exists in Python to make your life easier. It prevents you from absentmindedly creating a new variable in your `draw()` function (or any other function) that has the same name as a global variable, and overwriting the value in that global variable as a result.

If you forget to include the `global` keyword, your program might fail in various ways. You might get an "Unbound Local Error," which is Python's way of saying that you're attempting to use the value of a variable before having assigned a value to it. Alternatively, you might get no syntax errors at all, but your program's behavior will be strange: things that you intended to move will stay still. If either of these things happen, check to ensure that you've used the `global` keyword appropriately.

Click

In addition to the location of the mouse, Processing also keeps track of whether the mouse button is pressed. The `mousePressed` variable has a different value when the mouse button is pressed and when it is not. The `mousePressed` variable is a data type called `boolean`, which means that it has only two possible values: `True` and `False`. The value of `mousePressed` is `True` when a button is pressed.

Example 5-10: Click the Mouse

The mousePressed variable is used along with the if statement to determine when a line of code will run and when it won't. Try this example before we explain further:

```
def setup():
    size(240, 120)
    strokeWeight(30)

def draw():
    background(204)
    stroke(102)
    line(40, 0, 70, height)
    if mousePressed == True:
        stroke(0)
    line(0, 70, width, 50)
```

In this program, the code inside the if block runs only when a mouse button is pressed. When a button is not pressed, this code is ignored. Between the if keyword and the colon at the end of the line, there is a test expression that is evaluated to True or False:

```
if test:
    statements
```

When the test expression evaluates to True, the code inside the block is run; when the expression evaluates to False, the code inside the block is not run.

The == symbol compares the values on the left and right to test whether they are equivalent. This == symbol is different from the assignment operator, the single = symbol. The == symbol asks, "Are these things equal?" and the = symbol sets the value of a variable.

It's a common mistake, even for experienced programmers, to write = in your code when you mean to write ==. The Processing software won't always warn you when you do this, so be careful.

Alternatively, the test in draw() can be written like this:

```
if mousePressed:
```

Boolean variables, including mousePressed, don't need the explicit comparison with the == operator, because they can be only True or False.

Example 5-11: Detect When Not Clicked

A single if block gives you the choice of running some code or skipping it. You can extend an if block with an else block, allowing your program to choose between two options. The code inside the else block runs when the value of the if block test is false. For instance, the stroke color for a program can be white when the mouse button is not pressed, and can change to black when the button is pressed:

```
def setup():
    size(240, 120)
    strokeWeight(30)

def draw():
    background(204)
    stroke(102)
    line(40, 0, 70, height)
    if mousePressed:
        stroke(0)
```

```
else:
    stroke(255)
line(0, 70, width, 50)
```

Example 5-12: Multiple Mouse Buttons

Processing also tracks which button is pressed if you have more than one button on your mouse. The `mouseButton` variable can be one of three values: `LEFT`, `CENTER`, or `RIGHT`. To test which button was pressed, the `==` operator is needed, as shown here:

```
def setup():
    size(120, 120)
    strokeWeight(30)

def draw():
    background(204)
    stroke(102)
    line(40, 0, 70, height)
    if mousePressed:
        if mouseButton == LEFT:
            stroke(255)
        else:
            stroke(0)
        line(0, 70, width, 50)
```

A program can have many more `if` and `else` structures (see Figure 5-2) than those found in these short examples. They can be chained together into a long series with each testing for something different, and `if` blocks can be embedded inside of other `if` blocks to make more complex decisions.

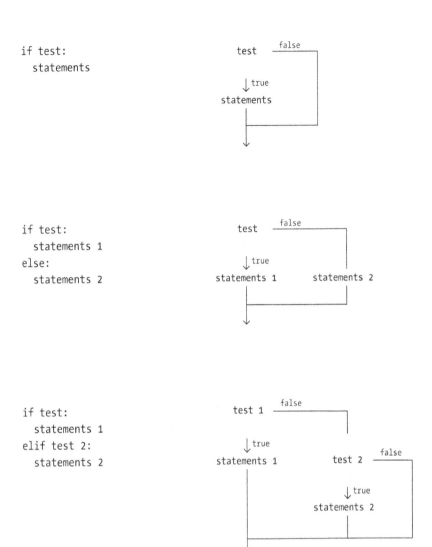

```
if test:
    statements
```

```
if test:
    statements 1
else:
    statements 2
```

```
if test:
    statements 1
elif test 2:
    statements 2
```

Figure 5-2. *The if and else structure makes decisions about which blocks of code to run*

Location

An **if** structure can be used with the **mouseX** and **mouseY** values to determine the location of the cursor within the window.

Example 5-13: Find the Cursor

For instance, this example tests to see whether the cursor is on the left or right side of a line and then moves the line toward the cursor:

```
x = 0.0

def setup():
  global x
  size(240, 120)
  x = width / 2

def draw():
  global x
  background(204)
  offset = 0
  if mouseX > x:
    x += 0.5
    offset = -10
  if mouseX < x:
    x -= 0.5
    offset = 10
  # Draw arrow left or right depending on "offset" value
  line(x, 0, x, height)
  line(mouseX, mouseY, mouseX + offset, mouseY - 10)
  line(mouseX, mouseY, mouseX + offset, mouseY + 10)
  line(mouseX, mouseY, mouseX + offset*3, mouseY)
```

To write programs that have graphical user interfaces (buttons, checkboxes, scrollbars, etc.), we need to write code that knows when the cursor is within an enclosed area of the screen. The following two examples introduce how to check whether the cursor is inside a circle and a rectangle. The code is written in a modular way with variables, so it can be used to check for *any* circle and rectangle by changing the values.

The test expressions in these `if` statements require further explanation. The expressions (`mouseX > x` and `mouseX < x`) are examples of *relational expressions*: expressions that compare two values with a relational operator. The most common relational operators are:

>	Greater than
<	Less than
>=	Greater than or equal to
<=	Less than or equal to
==	Equal to
!=	Not equal to

The relational expression always evaluates to `True` or `False`. For instance, the expression 5 > 3 is `True`. We can ask the question, "Is five greater than three?" Because the answer is "yes," we say the expression is `True`. For the expression 5 < 3, we ask, "Is five less than three?" Because the answer is "no," we say the expression is `False`. When the evaluation is `True`, the code inside the block is run, and when it's `False`, the code inside the block is not run.

Example 5-14: The Bounds of a Circle

For the circle test, we use the `dist()` function to get the distance from the center of the circle to the cursor, then we test to see if that distance is less than the radius of the circle (see Figure 5-3). If it is, we know we're inside. In this example, when the cursor is within the area of the circle, its size increases:

```
x = 120
y = 60
radius = 12
```

```
def setup():
  size(240, 120)
  ellipseMode(RADIUS)

def draw():
  global radius
  background(204)
  d = dist(mouseX, mouseY, x, y)
  if d < radius:
    radius += 1
    fill(0)
  else:
    fill(255)
  ellipse(x, y, radius, radius)
```

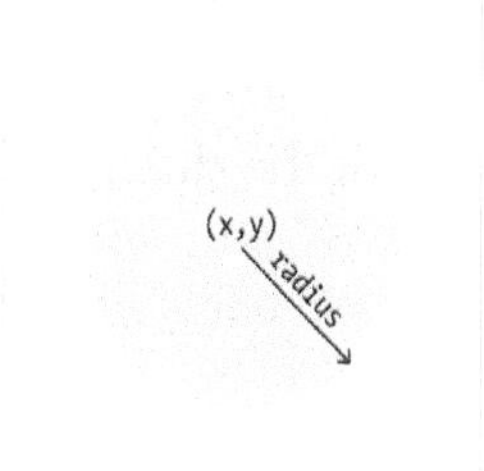

(x,y)

radius

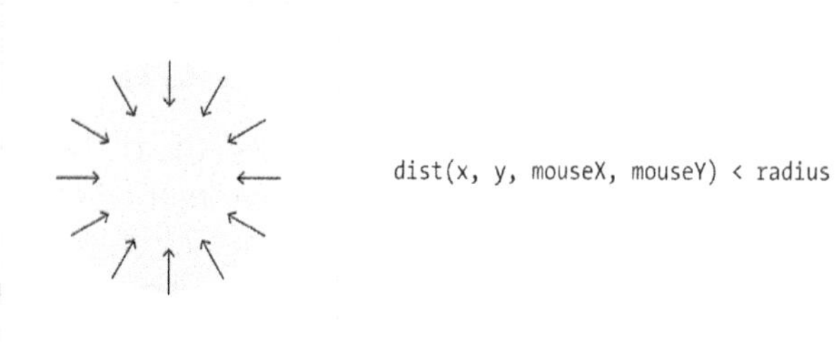

dist(x, y, mouseX, mouseY) < radius

Figure 5-3. *Circle rollover test. When the distance between the mouse and the circle is less than the radius, the mouse is inside the circle.*

Example 5-15: The Bounds of a Rectangle

We use another approach to test whether the cursor is inside a rectangle. We make four separate tests to check if the cursor is on the correct side of each edge of the rectangle, then we compare each test and if they are all **True**, we know the cursor is inside. This is illustrated in Figure 5-4. Each step is simple, but it looks complicated when it's all put together:

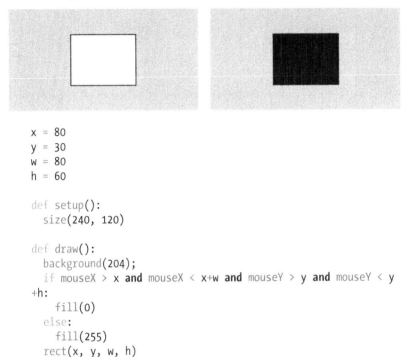

```
x = 80
y = 30
w = 80
h = 60

def setup():
  size(240, 120)

def draw():
  background(204);
  if mouseX > x and mouseX < x+w and mouseY > y and mouseY < y
+h:
    fill(0)
  else:
    fill(255)
  rect(x, y, w, h)
```

The test in the **if** statement is a little more complicated than we've seen. Four individual tests (e.g., **mouseX > x**) are combined with the logical AND operator, written with the keyword **and**, to ensure that every relational expression in the sequence is **True**. If one of them is **False**, the entire test is **False** and the fill color won't be set to black. This is explained further in the reference entry for **and**.

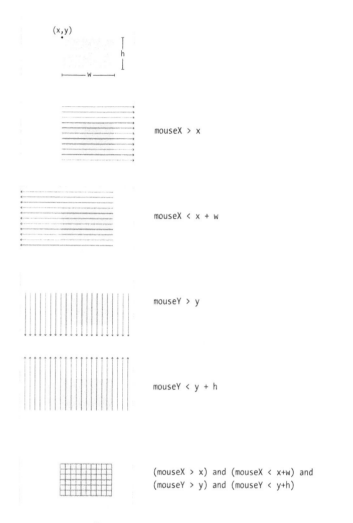

(x,y)

h

w

mouseX > x

mouseX < x + w

mouseY > y

mouseY < y + h

(mouseX > x) and (mouseX < x+w) and
(mouseY > y) and (mouseY < y+h)

Figure 5-4. *Rectangle rollover test. When all four tests are combined and true, the cursor is inside the rectangle.*

Type

Processing keeps track of when any key on a keyboard is pressed, as well as the last key pressed. Like the `mousePressed` variable, the `keyPressed` variable is `True` when any key is pressed, and `False` when no keys are pressed.

Example 5-16: Tap a Key

In this example, the second line is drawn only when a key is pressed:

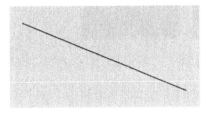 

```
def setup():
  size(240, 120)

def draw():
  background(204)
  line(20, 20, 220, 100)
  if keyPressed:
    line(220, 20, 20, 100)
```

The key variable stores the most recent key that has been pressed. The key variable holds a string value whose length is 1. Unlike the boolean variable keyPressed, which reverts to False each time a key is released, the key variable keeps its value until the next key is pressed. The following example uses the value of key to draw the character to the screen. Each time a new key is pressed, the value updates and a new character draws. Some keys, like Shift and Alt, don't have a visible character, so when you press them, nothing is drawn.

Example 5-17: Draw Some Letters

This example introduces the textSize() function to set the size of the letters, the textAlign() function to center the text on its x coordinate, and the text() function to draw the letter (these functions are discussed in more detail in "Fonts" on page 91):

```
def setup():
    size(120, 120)
    textSize(64)
    textAlign(CENTER)

def draw():
    background(0)
    if keyPressed:
        text(key, 60, 80)
```

Example 5-18: Check for Specific Keys

In this example, we test for an H or N to be typed. We use the comparison operator, the == symbol, to see if the key value is equal to the characters we're looking for:

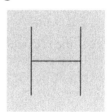

```
def setup():
    size(120, 120)

def draw():
    background(204)
    if keyPressed:
        if key == 'h' or key == 'H':
            line(30, 60, 90, 60)
        if key == 'n' or key == 'N':
            line(30, 20, 90, 100)
    line(30, 20, 30, 100)
    line(90, 20, 90, 100)
```

When we watch for H or N to be pressed, we need to check for both the lowercase and uppercase letters in the event that someone hits the Shift key or has the Caps Lock set. We combine the two tests together with a logical OR, using the or keyword. If we translate the second if statement in this example into plain language, it says, "If the h key is pressed OR the H key is pressed." Unlike with the logical AND (the and keyword), only one of these expressions need be True for the entire test to be True.

Some keys are more difficult to detect, because they aren't tied to a particular letter. Keys like Shift, Alt, and the arrow keys are *coded* and require an extra step to figure out if they are pressed. First, we need to check if the key that's been pressed is a coded key, then we check the code with the keyCode variable to see which key it is. The most frequently used keyCode values are ALT, CONTROL, and SHIFT, as well as the arrow keys, UP, DOWN, LEFT, and RIGHT.

Example 5-19: Move with Arrow Keys

The following example shows how to check for the left or right arrow keys to move a rectangle:

```
x = 215
def setup():
  size(480, 120)

def draw():
  global x
  if keyPressed and key == CODED:  # If it's a coded key
    if keyCode == LEFT:  # If it's the left arrow
      x -= 1
    elif keyCode == RIGHT:  # If it's the right arrow
      x += 1
  rect(x, 45, 50, 50)
```

This example illustrates the elif keyword, short for "else if." This keyword allows you to write an if structure that checks to see if more than one expression evaluates to true, flowing down to the next condition if the first condition evaluates to false. Translated into plain English, the inner if structure in this example translates as "if the keyCode is LEFT, then decrease x by one;

otherwise, if the `keyCode` is `RIGHT`, then increase x by one." You can use multiple `elif`s in one `if` structure, and `if` structures with `elif`s can include a final `else` clause as well.

Map

The numbers that are created by the mouse and keyboard often need to be modified to be useful within a program. For instance, if a sketch is 1920 pixels wide and the `mouseX` values are used to set the color of the background, the range of 0 to 1920 for `mouseX` might need to move into a range of 0 to 255 to better control the color. This transformation can be done with an equation or with a function called `map()`.

Example 5-20: Map Values to a Range

In this example, the location of two lines are controlled with the `mouseX` variable. The gray line is synchronized to the cursor position, but the black line stays closer to the center of the screen to move further away from the white line at the left and right edges:

```
def setup():
    size(240, 120)
    strokeWeight(12)

def draw():
    background(204)
    stroke(102)
    line(mouseX, 0, mouseX, height)  # Gray line
    stroke(0)
    mx = mouseX/2 + 60
    line(mx, 0, mx, height)  # Black line
```

The `map()` function is a more general way to make this type of change. It converts a variable from one range of numbers to another. The first parameter is the variable to be converted, the second and third parameters are the low and high values of that variable, and the fourth and fifth parameters are the desired low and high values. The `map()` function hides the math behind the conversion.

Example 5-21: Map with the map() Function

This example rewrites Example 5-20 on page 68 using `map()`:

```
def setup():
    size(240, 120)
    strokeWeight(12)

def draw():
    background(204)
    stroke(102)
    line(mouseX, 0, mouseX, height)   # Gray line
    stroke(0)
    mx = map(mouseX, 0, width, 60, 180)
    line(mx, 0, mx, height)  # Black line
```

The `map()` function makes the code easy to read, because the minimum and maximum values are clearly written as the parameters. In this example, values for `mouseX` between 0 and `width` are converted to a number from 60 (when `mouseX` is 0) up to 180 (when `mouseX` is equal to `width`). You'll find the useful `map()` function in many examples throughout this book. (If you're an experienced Python programmer, you'll recognize that Processing's `map()` function is different from Python's built-in `map()` function. This difference is discussed in "Built-In Function Names" on page 212.)

Robot 3: Response

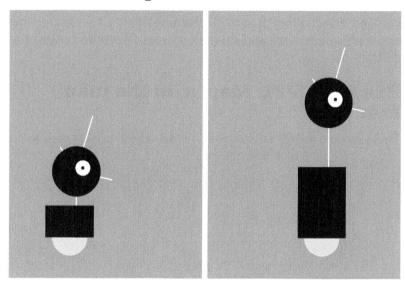

This program uses the variables introduced in Robot 2 (see "Robot 2: Variables" on page 45) and makes it possible to change them while the program runs so that the shapes respond to the mouse. The code inside the draw() block runs many times each second. At each frame, the variables defined in the program change in response to the mouseX and mouse Pressed variables.

The mouseX value controls the position of the robot with an easing technique so that movements are less instantaneous and feel more natural. When a mouse button is pressed, the values of neckHeight and bodyHeight change to make the robot short.

```
x = 60.0           # x coordinate
y = 440.0          # y coordinate
radius = 45        # Head radius
bodyHeight = 160   # Body height
neckHeight = 70    # Neck height

easing = 0.02

def setup():
    size(360, 480)
    strokeWeight(2)
```

```
ellipseMode(RADIUS)

def draw():
  global x
  targetX = mouseX
  x += (targetX - x) * easing

  if mousePressed:
    neckHeight = 16
    bodyHeight = 90
  else:
    neckHeight = 70
    bodyHeight = 160

  ny = y - bodyHeight - neckHeight - radius

  background(0, 153, 204)

  # Neck
  stroke(255)
  line(x+12, y-bodyHeight, x+12, ny)

  # Antennae
  line(x+12, ny, x-18, ny-43)
  line(x+12, ny, x+42, ny-99)
  line(x+12, ny, x+78, ny+15)

  # Body
  noStroke()
  fill(255, 204, 0)
  ellipse(x, y-33, 33, 33)
  fill(0)
  rect(x-45, y-bodyHeight, 90, bodyHeight-33)

  # Head
  fill(0)
  ellipse(x+12, ny, radius, radius)
  fill(255)
  ellipse(x+24, ny-6, 14, 14)
  fill(0)
  ellipse(x+24, ny-6, 3, 3)
```

6/Translate, Rotate, Scale

An alternative technique for positioning and moving things on screen is to change the screen coordinate system. For instance, you can move a shape 50 pixels to the right, or you can move the location of coordinate (0,0) 50 pixels to the right —the visual result on screen is the same.

By modifying the default coordinate system, we can create different *transformations* including *translation*, *rotation*, and *scaling*.

Translate

Working with transformations can be tricky, but the `translate()` function is the most straightforward, so we'll start with that. As Figure 6-1 shows, this function can shift the coordinate system left, right, up, and down.

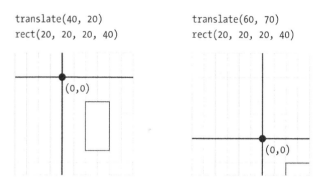
```
translate(40, 20)          translate(60, 70)
rect(20, 20, 20, 40)       rect(20, 20, 20, 40)
```

Figure 6-1. *Translating the coordinates*

Example 6-1: Translating Location

In this example, notice that the rectangle is drawn at coordinate (0,0), but it is moved around on the screen, because it is affected by `translate()`:

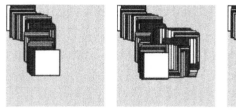

```
def setup():
    size(120, 120)

def draw():
    translate(mouseX, mouseY)
    rect(0, 0, 30, 30)
```

The `translate()` function sets the (0,0) coordinate of the screen to the mouse location (`mouseX` and `mouseY`). Each time the `draw()` block repeats, the `rect()` is drawn at the new origin, derived from the current mouse location.

Example 6-2: Multiple Translations

After a transformation is made, it is applied to all drawing functions that follow. Notice what happens when a second `translate` function is added to control a second rectangle:

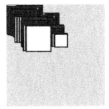  

```
def setup():
  size(120, 120)

def draw():
  translate(mouseX, mouseY)
  rect(0, 0, 30, 30)
  translate(35, 10)
  rect(0, 0, 15, 15)
```

The values for the `translate()` functions are added together. The smaller rectangle was translated the amount of mouseX + 35 and mouseY + 10. The x and y coordinates for both rectangles are (0,0), but the `translate()` functions move them to other positions on screen.

However, even though the transformations accumulate within the `draw()` block, they are reset each time `draw()` starts again at the top.

Rotate

The `rotate()` function rotates the coordinate system. It has one parameter, which is the angle (in radians) to rotate. It always rotates relative to (0,0), known as rotating around the origin. Refer back to Figure 3-2 to see the radians angle values. Figure 6-2 shows the difference between rotating with positive and negative numbers.

```
rotate(PI/12.0)
rect(20, 20, 20, 40)
```

```
rotate(-PI/3)
rect(20, 20, 20, 40)
```

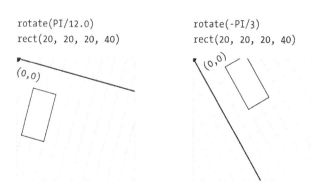

Figure 6-2. *Rotating the coordinates*

Example 6-3: Corner Rotation

To rotate a shape, first define the rotation angle with `rotate()`, then draw the shape. In this sketch, the amount to rotate (`mouseX / 100.0`) will be between 0 and 1.2 to define the rotation angle because `mouseX` will be between 0 and 120, the width of the Display Window specified with the `size()` command. Note that you should divide by 100.0 not 100, because of how numbers work in Python (see "Making Variables" on page 36).

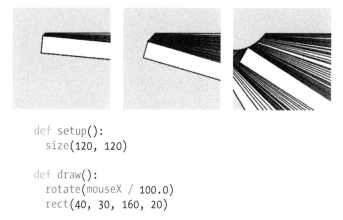

```
def setup():
    size(120, 120)

def draw():
    rotate(mouseX / 100.0)
    rect(40, 30, 160, 20)
```

Example 6-4: Center Rotation

To rotate a shape around its own center, it must be drawn with coordinate (0,0) in the middle. In this example, because the shape is 160 wide and 20 high as defined in `rect()`, it is drawn at the coordinate (-80, -10) to place (0,0) at the center of the shape:

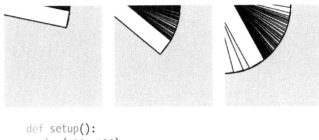

```
def setup():
    size(120, 120)

def draw():
    rotate(mouseX / 100.0)
    rect(-80, -10, 160, 20)
```

The previous pair of examples showed how to rotate around coordinate (0,0), but what about other possibilities? You can use the translate() and rotate() functions for more control. When they are combined, the order in which they appear affects the result. If the coordinate system is first moved and then rotated, that is different than first rotating the coordinate system, then moving it.

Example 6-5: Translation, Then Rotation

To spin a shape around its center point at a place on screen away from the origin, first use translate() to move to the location where you'd like the shape, then call rotate(), and then draw the shape with its center at coordinate (0,0):

```
angle = 0.0

def setup():
```

```
  size(120, 120)

def draw():
  global angle
  translate(mouseX, mouseY)
  rotate(angle)
  rect(-15, -15, 30, 30)
  angle += 0.1
```

Example 6-6: Rotation, Then Translation

The following example is identical to Example 6-5 on page 77, except that translate() and rotate() are reversed. The shape now rotates around the upper-left corner of the Display Window, with the distance from the corner set by translate():

 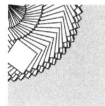 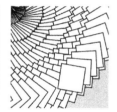

```
angle = 0.0

def setup():
  size(120, 120)

def draw():
  global angle
  rotate(angle)
  translate(mouseX, mouseY)
  rect(-15, -15, 30, 30)
  angle += 0.1
```

 Another option is to use the rectMode(), ellipse Mode(), imageMode(), and shapeMode() functions, which make it easier to draw shapes from their center. You can read about these functions in the *Processing Reference*.

Example 6-7: An Articulating Arm

In this example, we've put together a series of translate() and rotate() functions to create a linked arm that bends back and forth. Each translate() further moves the position of the lines, and each rotate() adds to the previous rotation to bend more:

```
angle = 0.0
angleDirection = 1
speed = 0.005

def setup():
  size(120, 120)

def draw():
  global angle, angleDirection
  background(204)
  translate(20, 25)   # Move to start position
  rotate(angle)
  strokeWeight(12)
  line(0, 0, 40, 0)
  translate(40, 0)    # Move to next joint
  rotate(angle * 2.0)
  strokeWeight(6)
  line(0, 0, 30, 0)
  translate(30, 0)    # Move to next joint
  rotate(angle * 2.5)
  strokeWeight(3)
  line(0, 0, 20, 0)
  angle += speed * angleDirection
  if angle > QUARTER_PI or angle < 0:
    angleDirection = -angleDirection
```

The angle variable grows from 0 to QUARTER_PI (one quarter of the value of pi), then decreases until it is less than zero, then the cycle repeats. The value of the angleDirection variable is always 1 or -1 to make the value of angle correspondingly increase or decrease.

Scale

The `scale()` function stretches the coordinates on the screen. Because the coordinates expand or contract as the scale changes, everything drawn to the Display Window increases or decreases in dimension. Use `scale(1.5)` to make everything 150% of their original size, or `scale(3)` to make them three times larger. Using `scale(1)` would have no effect, because everything would remain 100% of the original. To make things half their size, use `scale(0.5)`. See Figure 6-3 for an illustration of how the scale() function affects the coordinate system.

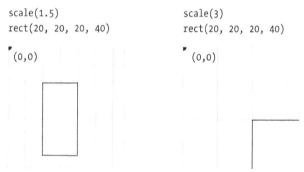

Figure 6-3. *Scaling the coordinates*

Example 6-8: Scaling

Like `rotate()`, the `scale()` function transforms from the origin. Therefore, as with `rotate()`, to scale a shape from its center, translate to its location, scale, and then draw with the center at coordinate (0,0):

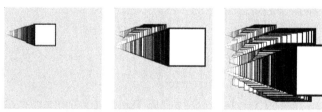

```
def setup():
    size(120, 120)

def draw():
```

```
translate(mouseX, mouseY)
scale(mouseX / 60.0)
rect(-15, -15, 30, 30)
```

Example 6-9: Keeping Strokes Consistent

From the thick lines in Example 6-8 on page 80, you can see how the `scale()` function affects the stroke weight. To maintain a consistent stroke weight as a shape scales, divide the desired stroke weight by the scalar value:

```
def setup():
  size(120, 120)

def draw():
  translate(mouseX, mouseY)
  scalar = mouseX / 60.0
  scale(scalar)
  if scalar > 0.0:
    strokeWeight(1.0 / scalar)
  else:
    strokeWeight(0)
  rect(-15, -15, 30, 30)
```

In this example, the value for the variable `scalar` might be zero if the value of `mouseX` is also zero (zero divided by 60 is zero). It's for this reason that we need to ensure that the value of `scalar` is greater than zero before performing the division to determine the appropriate stroke weight. Division by zero is an illegal operation in Python, and your program will immediately stop running if Python encounters a division expression where the divisor is zero.

Push and Pop

To isolate the effects of a transformation so they don't affect later commands, you can use the `pushMatrix()` and `popMatrix()` functions. When `pushMatrix()` is run, it saves a copy of the current coordinate system and then restores that system after `popMatrix()`. This is useful when transformations are needed for one shape but not wanted for another.

Example 6-10: Isolating Transformations

In this example, the smaller rectangle always draws in the same position because the translate(mouseX, mouseY) is cancelled by the popMatrix():

```
def setup():
  size(120, 120)

def draw():
  pushMatrix()
  translate(mouseX, mouseY)
  rect(0, 0, 30, 30)
  popMatrix()
  translate(35, 10)
  rect(0, 0, 15, 15)
```

 The pushMatrix() and popMatrix() functions are always used in pairs. For every pushMatrix(), you need to have a matching popMatrix().

Robot 4: Translate, Rotate, Scale

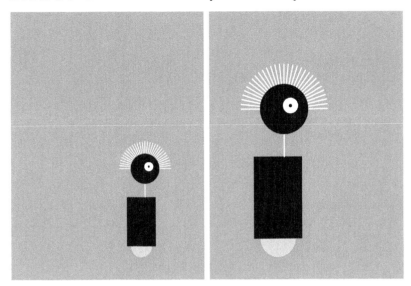

The `translate()`, `rotate()`, and `scale()` functions are all utilized in this modified robot sketch. In relation to "Robot 3: Response" on page 70, `translate()` is used to make the code easier to read. Here, notice how the x value no longer needs to be added to each drawing function because `translate()` moves everything.

Similarly, the `scale()` function is used to set the dimensions for the entire robot. When the mouse is not pressed, the size is set to 60% and when it is pressed, it goes to 100% in relation to the original coordinates. The `rotate()` function is used within a loop to draw a line, rotate it a little, then draw a second line, then rotate a little more, and so on until the loop has drawn 30 lines half-way around a circle to style a lovely head of robot hair:

```
x = 60              # x coordinate
y = 440             # y coordinate
radius = 45         # Head radius
bodyHeight = 180    # Body height
neckHeight = 40     # Neck height

easing = 0.04
```

```python
def setup():
  size(360, 480)
  strokeWeight(2)
  ellipseMode(RADIUS)

def draw():
  background(0, 153, 204)

  translate(mouseX, y)  # Move all to (mouseX, y)
  if mousePressed:
    scale(1.0)
  else:
    scale(0.6)  # 60% size when mouse is pressed

  # Body
  noStroke()
  fill(255, 204, 0)
  ellipse(0, -33, 33, 33)
  fill(0)
  rect(-45, -bodyHeight, 90, bodyHeight-33)

  # Neck
  stroke(255)
  neckY = -(bodyHeight + neckHeight + radius)
  line(12, -bodyHeight, 12, neckY)

  # Hair
  pushMatrix()
  translate(12, neckY)
  angle = -PI/30.0
  for i in range(31):
    line(80, 0, 0, 0)
    rotate(angle)
  popMatrix()

  # Head
  noStroke()
  fill(0)
  ellipse(12, neckY, radius, radius)
  fill(255)
  ellipse(24, neckY-6, 14, 14)
  fill(0)
  ellipse(24, neckY-6, 3, 3)
```

7/Media

Processing is capable of drawing more than simple lines and shapes. It's time to learn how to load raster images, vector files, and fonts into our programs to extend the visual possibilities to photography, detailed diagrams, and diverse typefaces.

Processing uses a folder named *data* to store such files, so that you never have to think about their location when moving sketches around and exporting them. We've posted some media files online for you to use in this chapter's examples (*http://www.processing.org/learning/books/media.zip*).

Download this file, unzip it to the desktop (or somewhere else convenient), and make a mental note of its location.

 To unzip on OS X, just double-click the file, and it will create a folder named *media*. On Windows, double-click the *media.zip* file, which will open a new window. In that window, drag the *media* folder to the desktop.

Create a new sketch, and select Add File from the Sketch menu. Find the *lunar.jpg* file from the media folder that you just unzipped and select it. To ensure that the file was added successfully, select Show Sketch Folder in the Sketch menu. You should see a folder named *data*, with a copy of *lunar.jpg* inside. When you add a file to the sketch, the *data* folder will automatically be created. Instead of using the Add File menu command, you can do the same thing by dragging files into the editor area of the Processing window. The files will be copied to the *data* folder the same way (and the *data* folder will be created if none exists).

You can also create the *data* folder outside of Processing and copy files there yourself. You won't get the message saying that files have been added, but this is a helpful method when you're working with large numbers of files.

 On Windows and OS X, extensions are hidden by default. It's a good idea to change that option so that you always see the full name of your files. On OS X, select Preferences from the Finder menu and then make sure "Show all filename extensions" is checked in the Advanced tab. On Windows, look for "Folder Options" and set the option there.

Images

There are three steps to follow before you can draw an image to the screen:

1. Add the image to the sketch's *data* folder (instructions given previously).
2. Create a variable to store the image.
3. Load the image into the variable with `loadImage()`.

Example 7-1: Load an Image

After all three steps are done, you can draw the image to the screen with the `image()` function. The first parameter to `image()` specifies the image to draw; the second and third set the *x* and *y* coordinates:

```
img = None

def setup():
    global img
    size(480, 120)
    img = loadImage("lunar.jpg")

def draw():
    image(img, 0, 0)
```

Optional fourth and fifth parameters to the image function set the width and height to draw the image. If the fourth and fifth parameters are not used, the image is drawn at the size at which it was created.

Note that we've initialized the img variable in the preceding example to the value None, which is a special placeholder value in Python that allows us to create a variable but leave it "empty." It's only later, in setup, that we call the loadImage function and assign a real value to the img variable. (This variable assignment dance is necessary because the loadImage function—and many of the other functions for loading and creating media resources discussed in this chapter—can't be called until after setup is called.)

These next examples show how to work with more than one image in the same program and how to resize an image.

Example 7-2: Load More Images

For this example, you'll need to add the *capsule.jpg* file (found in the *media* folder you downloaded) to your sketch using one of the methods described earlier:

```
img1 = None
img2 = None

def setup():
    global img1, img2
    size(480, 120)
    img1 = loadImage("lunar.jpg")
    img2 = loadImage("capsule.jpg")

def draw():
    image(img1, -120, 0)
    image(img1, 130, 0, 240, 120)
    image(img2, 300, 0, 240, 120)
```

Example 7-3: Mousing Around with Images

When the `mouseX` and `mouseY` values are used as part of the fourth and fifth parameters of `image()`, the image size changes as the mouse moves:

```
img = None

def setup():
    global img
    size(480, 120)
    img = loadImage("lunar.jpg")

def draw():
```

```
background(0)
image(img, 0, 0, mouseX * 2, mouseY * 2)
```

 When an image is displayed larger or smaller than its actual size, it may become distorted. Be careful to prepare your images at the sizes they will be used. When the display size of an image is changed with the image() function, the actual image on the hard drive doesn't change.

Processing can load and display raster images in the JPEG, PNG, and GIF formats. (Vector shapes in the SVG format can be displayed in a different way, as described in "Shapes" on page 94.) You can convert images to the JPEG, PNG, and GIF formats using programs like GIMP and Photoshop. Digital cameras typically save JPEG images that are much larger than the drawing area of most Processing sketches, so resizing such images before they are added to the *data* folder will make your sketches run more efficiently.

GIF and PNG images support transparency, which means that pixels can be invisible or partially visible (recall the discussion of color() and alpha values in Example 3-17 on page 26). GIF images have 1-bit transparency, which means that pixels are either fully opaque or fully transparent. PNG images have 8-bit transparency, which means that each pixel can have a variable level of opacity. The following examples show the difference, using the *clouds.gif* and *clouds.png* files found in the *media* folder that you downloaded. Be sure to add them to the sketch before trying each example.

Example 7-4: Transparency with a GIF

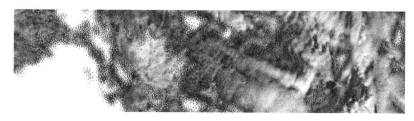

```
img = None

def setup():
    global img
    size(480, 120)
    img = loadImage("clouds.gif")

def draw():
    background(255)
    image(img, 0, 0)
    image(img, 0, mouseY * -1)
```

Example 7-5: Transparency with a PNG

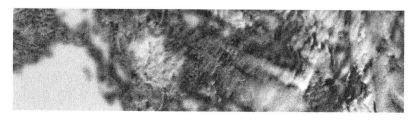

```
img = None

def setup():
    global img
    size(480, 120)
    img = loadImage("clouds.png")

def draw():
    background(255)
    image(img, 0, 0)
    image(img, 0, mouseY * -1)
```

Remember to include the file extensions *.gif*, *.jpg*, or *.png* when you load the image. Also, be sure that the image name is typed exactly as it appears in the file, including the case of the letters. And if you missed it, read the note earlier in this chapter about making sure that the file extensions are visible on OS X and Windows.

Fonts

The Processing software can display text using TrueType (*.ttf*) and OpenType (*.otf*) fonts, as well as a custom bitmap format called VLW. For this introduction, we will load a TrueType font from the *data* folder, the *SourceCodePro-Regular.ttf* font included in the *media* folder that you downloaded earlier.

The following websites are good places to find fonts with open licenses to use with Processing:

- http://www.google.com/fonts
- http://openfontlibrary.org
- http://www.theleagueofmoveabletype.com

Now it's possible to load the font and add words to a sketch. This part is similar to working with images, but there's one extra step:

1. Add the font to the sketch's *data* folder (instructions given previously).
2. Create a variable to store the font.
3. Create the font and assign it to a variable with `createFont()`. This reads the font file, and creates a version of it at a specific size that can be used by Processing.
4. Use the `textFont()` command to set the current font.

Example 7-6: Drawing with Fonts

Now you can draw these letters to the screen with the `text()` function, and you can change the size with `textSize()`:

That's one small step fo

That's one small step for man...

```
font = None

def setup():
    global font
    size(480, 120)
    font = createFont("SourceCodePro-Regular.ttf", 32)
    textFont(font)

def draw():
    background(102)
    textSize(32)
    text("That's one small step for man...", 25, 60)
    textSize(16)
    text("That's one small step for man...", 27, 90)
```

The first parameter to `text()` is the character(s) to draw to the screen. (Notice that the characters are enclosed within quotes.) The second and third parameters set the horizontal and vertical location. The location is relative to the baseline of the text (see Figure 7-1).

(x,y)

Figure 7-1. *Typography coordinates*

Example 7-7: Draw Text in a Box

You can also set text to draw inside a box by adding fourth and fifth parameters that specify the width and height of the box:

```
font = None

def setup():
  global font
  size(480, 120)
  font = createFont("SourceCodePro-Regular.ttf", 24)
  textFont(font)

def draw():
  background(102)
  text("That's one small step for man...", 26, 24, 240, 100)
```

Example 7-8: Store Text in a String

In the previous example, the words inside the text() function start to make the code difficult to read. We can store these words in a variable to make the code more modular. The string data type is used to store text data. Here's a new version of the previous example that uses a string:

```
font = None
quote = "That's one small step for man..."

def setup():
  global font
  size(480, 120)
  font = createFont("SourceCodePro-Regular.ttf", 24)
  textFont(font)

def draw():
  background(102)
  text(quote, 26, 24, 240, 100)
```

There's a set of additional functions that affect how letters are displayed on screen. They are explained, with examples, in the Typography category of the *Processing Reference*.

Shapes

If you make vector shapes in a program like Inkscape or Illustrator, you can load them into Processing directly. This is helpful for shapes you'd rather not build with Processing's drawing functions. As with images, you need to add them to your sketch before they can be loaded.

There are three steps to load and draw an SVG file:

1. Add an SVG file to the sketch's *data* folder.
2. Create a variable to store the vector file.
3. Load the vector file into the variable with `loadShape()`.

Example 7-9: Draw with Shapes

After following these steps, you can draw the image to the screen with the `shape()` function:

```
network = None

def setup():
    global network
    size(480, 120)
    network = loadShape("network.svg")

def draw():
    background(0)
    shape(network, 30, 10)
    shape(network, 180, 10, 280, 280)
```

The parameters for shape() are similar to image(). The first parameter tells shape() which SVG to draw, and the next pair sets the position. Optional fourth and fifth parameters set the width and height.

Example 7-10: Scaling Shapes

Unlike raster images, vector shapes can be scaled to any size without losing resolution. In this example, the shape is scaled based on the mouseX variable, and the shapeMode() function is used to draw the shape from its center, rather than the default position, the upper-left corner:

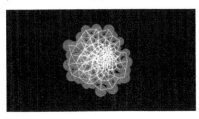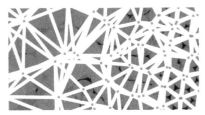

```
network = None

def setup():
  global network
  size(240, 120)
  shapeMode(CENTER)
  network = loadShape("network.svg")

def draw():
  background(0)
  diameter = map(mouseX, 0, width, 10, 800)
  shape(network, 120, 60, diameter, diameter)
```

 Processing doesn't support all SVG features. See the reference entry for PShape for more details.

Example 7-11: Creating a New Shape

In addition to loading shapes through the data folder, new shapes can be created with code through the createShape() function. In the next example, one of the creatures from Example 3-21 on page 29 is built in the **setup()**. Once this happens, the shape can be used anywhere in the program with the **shape()** function:

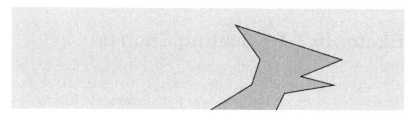

```
dino = None

def setup():
    global dino
    size(480, 120)
    dino = createShape()
    dino.beginShape()
    dino.fill(153, 176, 180)
    dino.vertex(50, 120)
    dino.vertex(100, 90)
    dino.vertex(110, 60)
    dino.vertex(80, 20)
    dino.vertex(210, 60)
    dino.vertex(160, 80)
    dino.vertex(200, 90)
    dino.vertex(140, 100)
    dino.vertex(130, 120)
    dino.endShape()

def draw():
    background(204)
    translate(mouseX - 120, 0)
    shape(dino, 0, 0)
```

Making a custom PShape with **createShape()** can make sketches more efficient when the same shape is drawn many times.

Robot 5: Media

Unlike the robots created from lines and rectangles drawn in Processing in the previous chapters, these robots were created with a vector drawing program. For some shapes, it's often easier to point and click in a software tool like Inkscape or Illustrator than to define the shapes with coordinates in code.

There's a trade-off to selecting one image creation technique over another. When shapes are defined in Processing, there's more flexibility to modify them while the program is running. If the shapes are defined elsewhere and then loaded into Processing, changes are limited to the position, angle, and size. When loading each robot from an SVG file, as this example shows, the variations featured in Robot 2 (see "Robot 2: Variables" on page 45) are impossible.

Images can be loaded into a program to bring in visuals created in other programs or captured with a camera. With this image in the background, our robots are now exploring for life forms in Norway at the dawn of the 20th century.

The SVG and PNG file used in this example can be downloaded from http://www.processing.org/learning/books/media.zip:

```python
bot1 = None
bot2 = None
bot3 = None
landscape = None

easing = 0.05
offset = 0

def setup():
    global bot1, bot2, bot3, landscape
    size(720, 480)
    bot1 = loadShape("robot1.svg")
    bot2 = loadShape("robot2.svg")
    bot3 = loadShape("robot3.svg")
    landscape = loadImage("alpine.png")

def draw():
    global offset

    # Set the background to the "landscape" image; this image
    # must be the same width and height as the program
    background(landscape)

    # Set the left/right offset and apply easing to make
    # the transition smooth
    targetOffset = map(mouseY, 0, height, -40, 40)
    offset += (targetOffset - offset) * easing

    # Draw the left robot
    shape(bot1, 85 + offset, 65)

    # Draw the right robot smaller and give it a smaller offset
    smallerOffset = offset * 0.7
    shape(bot2, 510 + smallerOffset, 140, 78, 248)

    # Draw the smallest robot, give it a smaller offset
    smallerOffset *= -0.5;
    shape(bot3, 410 + smallerOffset, 225, 39, 124)
```

8/Motion

Like a flip book, animation on screen is created by drawing an image, then drawing a slightly different image, then another, and so on. The illusion of fluid motion is created by *persistence of vision*. When a set of similar images is presented at a fast enough rate, our brains translate these images into motion.

Frames

To create smooth motion, Processing tries to run the code inside `draw()` at 60 frames each second. A *frame* is one trip through the `draw()` and the *frame rate* is how many frames are drawn each second. Therefore, a program that draws 60 frames each second means the program runs the entire code inside `draw()` 60 times each second.

Example 8-1: See the Frame Rate

To confirm the frame rate, run this program and watch the values print to the Console. The `frameRate` variable keeps track of the program's speed:

```
def draw():
    print frameRate
```

Example 8-2: Set the Frame Rate

The `frameRate()` function changes the speed at which the program runs. To see the result, uncomment different versions of `frameRate()` in this example:

```
def setup():
    frameRate(30)    # Thirty frames each second
    #frameRate(12)   # Twelve frames each second
    #frameRate(2)    # Two frames each second
    #frameRate(0.5)  # One frame every two seconds

def draw():
    print frameRate
```

 Processing *tries* to run the code at 60 frames each second, but if it takes longer than 1/60th of a second to run the `draw()` method, then the frame rate will decrease. The `frameRate()` function specifies only the maximum frame rate, and the actual frame rate for any program depends on the computer that is running the code.

Speed and Direction

To create fluid motion examples, we use a data type called `float`. This type of variable stores numbers with decimal places, which provide more resolution for working with motion. For instance, when using `int`s, the slowest you can move each frame is one pixel at a time (1, 2, 3, 4, . . .), but with `float`s, you can move as slowly as you want (1.01, 1.01, 1.02, 1.03, . . .).

The data type of a variable depends on the value that you assign to it. To create a value of type `float`, include a decimal point as part of the number in your code. If you don't include a decimal point, Python will create a value of type `int`. In the following code snippet, for example, the data type of variable `var1` is `float`, whereas the data type of variable `var2` is `int`:

```
var1 = 12.5 # float
var2 = 4    # int
```

In Python, you can write arithmetic expressions that mix `ints` and `floats` (e.g., `6 * 0.5`). The data type that results from such expressions is always `float`.

Example 8-3: Move a Shape

The following example moves a shape from left to right by updating the x variable:

```
radius = 40.0
x = -radius
speed = 0.5

def setup():
    size(240, 120)
    ellipseMode(RADIUS)

def draw():
    global x
    background(0)
    x += speed # Increase the value of x
    arc(x, 60, radius, radius, 0.52, 5.76)
```

When you run this code, you'll notice the shape moves off the right of the screen when the value of the x variable is greater than the width of the window. The value of x continues to increase, but the shape is no longer visible.

Example 8-4: Wrap Around

There are many alternatives to this behavior, which you can choose from according to your preference. First, we'll extend the code to show how to move the shape back to the left edge of the screen after it disappears off the right. In this case, picture the screen as a flattened cylinder, with the shape moving around the outside to return to its starting point:

```
radius = 40.0
x = -radius
speed = 0.5

def setup():
    size(240, 120)
    ellipseMode(RADIUS)

def draw():
    global x
    background(0)
    x += speed                  # Increase the value of x
    if x > width+radius:        # If the shape is off screen,
        x = -radius             # move to the left edge
    arc(x, 60, radius, radius, 0.52, 5.76)
```

On each trip through draw(), the code tests to see if the value of x has increased beyond the width of the screen (plus the radius of the shape). If it has, we set the value of x to a negative value, so that as it continues to increase, it will enter the screen from the left. See Figure 8-1 for a diagram of how it works.

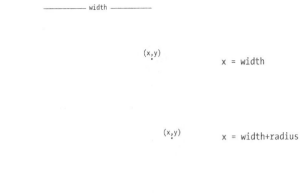

width

(x,y)   x = width

(x,y)   x = width+radius

(x,y)   x = -radius

Figure 8-1. *Testing for the edges of the window*

Example 8-5: Bounce Off the Wall

In this example, we'll extend Example 8-3 on page 101 to have the shape change directions when it hits an edge, instead of wrapping around to the left. To make this happen, we add a new variable to store the direction of the shape. A direction value of 1 moves the shape to the right, and a value of −1 moves the shape to the left:

```
radius = 40.0
x = 110.0
speed = 0.5
direction = 1

def setup():
  size(240, 120)
  ellipseMode(RADIUS)
```

```
def draw():
  global x, direction
  background(0)
  x += speed * direction
  if x > width-radius or x < radius:
    direction = -direction # Flip direction
  if direction == 1:
    arc(x, 60, radius, radius, 0.52, 5.76) # Face right
  else:
    arc(x, 60, radius, radius, 3.67, 8.9)  # Face left
```

When the shape reaches an edge, this code flips the shape's direction by changing the sign of the direction variable. For example, if the direction variable is positive when the shape reaches an edge, the code flips it to negative.

Tweening

Sometimes you want to animate a shape to go from one point on screen to another. With a few lines of code, you can set up the start position and the stop position, then calculate the in-between (*tween*) positions at each frame.

Example 8-6: Calculate Tween Positions

To make this example code modular, we've created a group of variables at the top. Run the code a few times and change the values to see how this code can move a shape from any location to any other at a range of speeds. Change the step variable to alter the speed:

```
startX = 20.0      # Initial x coordinate
stopX = 160.0      # Final x coordinate
startY = 30.0      # Initial y coordinate
stopY = 80.0       # Final y coordinate
x = startX         # Current x coordinate
```

```
y = startY          # Current y coordinate
step = 0.005        # Size of each step (0.0 to 1.0)
pct = 0.0           # Percentage traveled (0.0 to 1.0)

def setup():
  size(240, 120)

def draw():
  global x, y, pct
  background(0)
  if pct < 1.0:
    x = startX + ((stopX-startX) * pct)
    y = startY + ((stopY-startY) * pct)
    pct += step
  ellipse(x, y, 20, 20)
```

Random

Unlike the smooth, linear motion common to computer graph-ics, motion in the physical world is usually idiosyncratic. For instance, think of a leaf floating to the ground, or an ant crawling over rough terrain. We can simulate the unpredictable qualities of the world by generating random numbers. The random() func-tion calculates these values; we can set a range to tune the amount of disarray in a program.

Example 8-7: Generate Random Values

The following short example prints random values to the Con-sole, with the range limited by the position of the mouse. As you can see when you run the example, the random() function always returns a floating-point value:

```
def draw():
  r = random(0, mouseX)
  print r
```

Note that the random() function is a Processing function, and behaves differently from the random module included in the Python standard library. See "Python Standard Library" on page 213 for more information.

Example 8-8: Draw Randomly

The following example builds on Example 8-7 on page 105; it uses the values from `random()` to change the position of lines on screen. When the mouse is at the left of the screen, the change is small; as it moves to the right, the values from `random()` increase and the movement becomes more exaggerated. Because the `random()` function is inside the `for` loop, a new random value is calculated for each point of every line:

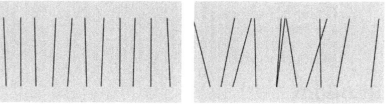

```
def setup():
    size(240, 120)

def draw():
    background(204)
    for x in range(20, width, 20):
        mx = mouseX / 10
        offsetA = random(-mx, mx)
        offsetB = random(-mx, mx)
        line(x + offsetA, 20, x - offsetB, 100)
```

Example 8-9: Move Shapes Randomly

When used to move shapes around on screen, random values can generate images that are more natural in appearance. In the following example, the position of the circle is modified by random values on each trip through `draw()`. Because the `background()` function is not used, past locations are traced:

```
speed = 2.5
diameter = 20
x = 0.0
y = 0.0

def setup():
  global x, y
  size(240, 120)
  x = width/2
  y = height/2

def draw():
  global x, y
  x += random(-speed, speed)
  y += random(-speed, speed)
  ellipse(x, y, diameter, diameter)
```

If you watch this example long enough, you may see the circle leave the window and come back. This is left to chance, but we could add a few **if** structures or use the **constrain()** function to keep the circle from leaving the screen. The **constrain()** function limits a value to a specific range, which can be used to keep x and y within the boundaries of the Display Window. By replacing the **draw()** in the preceding code with the following, you'll ensure that the ellipse will remain on the screen:

```
def draw():
  global x, y
  x += random(-speed, speed)
  y += random(-speed, speed)
  x = constrain(x, 0, width)
  y = constrain(y, 0, height)
  ellipse(x, y, diameter, diameter)
```

The **randomSeed()** function can be used to force **random()** to produce the same sequence of numbers each time a program is run. This is described further in the *Processing Reference*.

Timers

Every Processing program counts the amount of time that has passed since it was started. It counts in milliseconds (thousandths of a second), so after 1 second, the counter is at 1,000; after 5 seconds, it's at 5,000; and after 1 minute, it's at 60,000. We can use this counter to trigger animations at specific times. The `millis()` function returns this counter value.

Example 8-10: Time Passes

You can watch the time pass when you run this program:

```
def draw():
    timer = millis()
    print timer
```

Example 8-11: Triggering Timed Events

When paired with an `if` block, the values from `millis()` can be used to sequence animation and events within a program. For instance, after two seconds have elapsed, the code inside the `if` block can trigger a change. In this example, variables called `time1` and `time2` determine when to change the value of the `x` variable:

```
time1 = 2000
time2 = 4000
x = 0.0

def setup():
    size(480, 120)

def draw():
    global x
    currentTime = millis()
    background(204)
    if currentTime > time2:
        x -= 0.5
    elif currentTime > time1:
        x += 2
    ellipse(x, 60, 90, 90)
```

Circular

If you're a trigonometry ace, you already know how amazing the sine and cosine functions are. If you're not, we hope the next examples will trigger your interest. We won't discuss the math in detail here, but we'll show a few applications to generate fluid motion.

Figure 8-2 shows a visualization of sine wave values and how they relate to angles. At the top and bottom of the wave, notice how the rate of change (the change on the vertical axis) slows down, stops, then switches direction. It's this quality of the curve that generates interesting motion.

The `sin()` and `cos()` functions in Processing return values between −1 and 1 for the sine or cosine of the specified angle. Like `arc()`, the angles must be given in radian values (see Example 3-7 on page 18 and Example 3-8 on page 19 for a reminder of how radians work). To be useful for drawing, the `float` values returned by `sin()` and `cos()` are usually multiplied by a larger value.

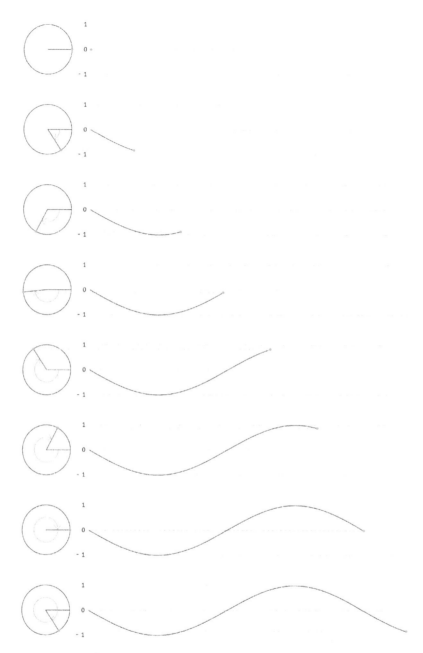

Figure 8-2. *A sine wave is created by tracing the sine values of an angle that moves around a circle*

Example 8-12: Sine Wave Values

This example shows how values for sin() cycle from −1 to 1 as the angle increases. With the map() function, the sinval variable is converted from this range to values from 0 and 255. This new value is used to set the background color of the window:

```
angle = 0.0

def draw():
  global angle
  sinval = sin(angle)
  print sinval
  gray = map(sinval, -1, 1, 0, 255)
  background(gray)
  angle += 0.1
```

Example 8-13: Sine Wave Movement

This example shows how these values can be converted into movement:

 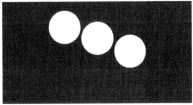

```
angle = 0.0
offset = 60.0
scalar = 40.0
speed = 0.05

def setup():
  size(240, 120)

def draw():
  global angle
  background(0)
  y1 = offset + sin(angle) * scalar
  y2 = offset + sin(angle + 0.4) * scalar
  y3 = offset + sin(angle + 0.8) * scalar
  ellipse( 80, y1, 40, 40)
  ellipse(120, y2, 40, 40)
```

```
ellipse(160, y3, 40, 40)
angle += speed
```

Example 8-14: Circular Motion

When sin() and cos() are used together, they can produce circular motion. The cos() values provide the *x* coordinates, and the sin() values provide the *y* coordinates. Both are multiplied by a variable named scalar to change the radius of the movement and summed with an offset value to set the center of the circular motion:

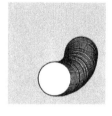  

```
angle = 0.0
offset = 60.0
scalar = 30.0
speed = 0.05

def setup():
    size(120, 120)

def draw():
    global angle
    x = offset + cos(angle) * scalar
    y = offset + sin(angle) * scalar
    ellipse( x, y, 40, 40)
    angle += speed
```

Example 8-15: Spirals

A slight change made to increase the scalar value at each frame produces a spiral, rather than a circle:

```
angle = 0.0
offset = 60.0
scalar = 2.0
speed = 0.05

def setup():
  size(120, 120)
  fill(0)

def draw():
  global angle, scalar
  x = offset + cos(angle) * scalar;
  y = offset + sin(angle) * scalar;
  ellipse( x, y, 2, 2)
  angle += speed
  scalar += speed
```

Robot 6: Motion

In this example, the techniques for random and circular motion are applied to the robot. The `background()` was removed to make it easier to see how the robot's position and body change.

At each frame, a random number between −4 and 4 is added to the x coordinate, and a random number between −1 and 1 is added to the y coordinate. This causes the robot to move more from left to right than top to bottom. Numbers calculated from the `sin()` function change the height of the neck so it oscillates between 50 and 110 pixels high:

```
x = 180.0              # x coordinate
y = 400.0              # y coordinate
bodyHeight = 153.0     # Body height
neckHeight = 56.0      # Neck height
radius = 45.0          # Head radius
angle = 0.0            # Angle for motion

def setup():
    size(360, 480)
    ellipseMode(RADIUS)
    background(0, 153, 204)
```

```
def draw():
  global x, y, angle
  # Change position by a small random amount
  x += random(-4, 4)
  y += random(-1, 1)

  # Change height of neck
  neckHeight = 80 + sin(angle) * 30
  angle += 0.05

  # Adjust the height of the head
  ny = y - bodyHeight - neckHeight - radius

  # Neck
  stroke(102)
  line(x+2, y-bodyHeight, x+2, ny)
  line(x+12, y-bodyHeight, x+12, ny)
  line(x+22, y-bodyHeight, x+22, ny)

  # Antennae
  line(x+12, ny, x-18, ny-43)
  line(x+12, ny, x+42, ny-99)
  line(x+12, ny, x+78, ny+15)

  # Body
  noStroke()
  fill(255, 204, 0)
  ellipse(x, y-33, 33, 33)
  fill(0)
  rect(x-45, y-bodyHeight, 90, bodyHeight-33)
  fill(102)
  rect(x-45, y-bodyHeight+17, 90, 6)

  # Head
  fill(0)
  ellipse(x+12, ny, radius, radius)
  fill(255)
  ellipse(x+24, ny-6, 14, 14)
  fill(0)
  ellipse(x+24, ny-6, 3, 3)
```

9/Functions

Functions are the basic building blocks for Processing programs. They have appeared in every example we've presented. For instance, we've frequently used the `size()` function, the `line()` function, and the `fill()` function. This chapter shows how to write new functions to extend the capabilities of Processing beyond its built-in features.

The power of functions is modularity. Functions are independent software units that are used to build more complex programs—like LEGO bricks, where each type of brick serves a specific purpose, and making a complex model requires using the different parts together. As with functions, the true power of these bricks is the ability to build many different forms from the same set of elements. The same group of LEGOs that makes a spaceship can be reused to construct a truck, a skyscraper, and many other objects.

Functions are helpful if you want to draw a more complex shape like a tree over and over. The function to draw the tree shape would be made up of Processing's built-in commands, like `line()`, which create the form. After the code to draw the tree is written, you don't need to think about the details of tree drawing again—you can simply write `tree()` (or whatever you named the function) to draw the shape. Functions allow a complex sequence of statements to be abstracted, so you can focus on the higher-level goal (such as drawing a tree), and not the details of the implementation (the `line()` commands that define the tree shape). Once a function is defined, the code inside the function need not be repeated again.

Function Basics

A computer runs a program one line at a time. When a function is run, the computer jumps to where the function is defined and runs the code there, then jumps back to where it left off.

Example 9-1: Roll the Dice

This behavior is illustrated with the `rollDice()` function written for this example. When a program starts, it runs the code in `setup()` and then stops. The program takes a detour and runs the code inside `rollDice()` each time it appears:

```
def setup():
    print "Ready to roll!"
    rollDice(20)
    rollDice(20)
    rollDice(6)
    print "Finished."

def rollDice(numSides):
    d = 1 + int(random(numSides))
    print "Rolling...", d
```

The two lines of code in `rollDice()` select a random number between 1 and the number of sides on the dice, and prints that number to the Console. Because the numbers are random, you'll see different numbers each time the program is run:

```
Ready to roll!
Rolling... 8
Rolling... 13
Rolling... 2
Finished.
```

Each time the `rollDice()` function is run inside `setup()`, the code within the function runs from top to bottom, then the program continues on the next line within `setup()`.

The `random()` function (described in Example 8-7 on page 105) returns a number from 0 up to (but not including) the number specified. So `random(6)` returns a number between 0 and

5.99999.... Because `random()` returns a `float` value, we also use `int()` to convert it to an integer. So `int(random(6))` will return 0, 1, 2, 3, 4, or 5. Then we add 1 so that the number returned is between 1 and 6 (like a die). Like many other cases in this book, counting from 0 makes it easier to use the results of `random()` with other calculations.

Example 9-2: Another Way to Roll

If an equivalent program were written without the `rollDice()` function, it might look like this:

```
def setup():
    print "Ready to roll!"
    d1 = 1 + int(random(20))
    print "Rolling...", d1
    d2 = 1 + int(random(20))
    print "Rolling...", d2
    d3 = 1 + int(random(6))
    print "Rolling...", d3
    print "Finished."
```

The `rollDice()` function in Example 9-1 on page 118 makes the code easier to read and maintain. The program is clearer because the name of the function clearly states its purpose. In this example, we see the `random()` function in `setup()`, but its use is not as obvious. The number of sides on the die is also clearer with a function: when the code says `rollDice(6)`, it's obvious that it's simulating the roll of a six-sided die. Also, Example 9-1 on page 118 is easier to maintain, because information is not repeated. The phrase `Rolling...` is repeated three times here. If you want to change that text to something else, you would need to update the program in three places, rather than making a single edit inside the `rollDice()` function. In addition, as you'll see in Example 9-5 on page 122, a function can also make a program much shorter (and therefore easier to maintain and read), which helps reduce the potential number of bugs.

Make a Function

In this section, we'll draw an owl to explain the steps involved in making a function.

Example 9-3: Draw the Owl

First, we'll draw the owl without using a function:

```
def setup():
    size(480, 120)

def draw():
    background(176, 204, 226)
    translate(110, 110)
    stroke(138, 138, 125)
    strokeWeight(70)
    line(0, -35, 0, -65)   # Body
    noStroke()
    fill(255)
    ellipse(-17.5, -65, 35, 35) # Left eye dome
    ellipse(17.5, -65, 35, 35)  # Right eye dome
    arc(0, -65, 70, 70, 0, PI)  # Chin
    fill(51, 51, 30)
    ellipse(-14, -65, 8, 8)     # Left eye
    ellipse(14, -65, 8, 8)      # Right eye
    quad(0, -58, 4, -51, 0, -44, -4, -51)   # Beak
```

Notice that `translate()` is used to move the origin (0,0) to 110 pixels over and 110 pixels down. Then the owl is drawn relative to (0,0), with its coordinates sometimes positive and negative as it's centered around the new 0,0 point. See Figure 9-1.

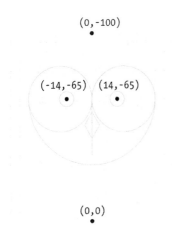

(0,-100)

(-14,-65) (14,-65)

(0,0)

Figure 9-1. *The owl's coordinates*

Example 9-4: Two's Company

The code presented in Example 9-3 on page 120 is reasonable if there is only one owl, but when we draw a second, the length of the code is nearly doubled:

```
def setup():
  size(480, 120)

def draw():
  background(176, 204, 226)

  # Left owl
  translate(110, 110)
  stroke(138, 138, 125)
  strokeWeight(70)
  line(0, -35, 0, -65)  # Body
  noStroke()
  fill(255)
```

```
ellipse(-17.5, -65, 35, 35) # Left eye dome
ellipse(17.5, -65, 35, 35)  # Right eye dome
arc(0, -65, 70, 70, 0, PI)  # Chin
fill(51, 51, 30)
ellipse(-14, -65, 8, 8)     # Left eye
ellipse(14, -65, 8, 8)      # Right eye
quad(0, -58, 4, -51, 0, -44, -4, -51)  # Beak

# Right owl
translate(70, 0);
stroke(138, 138, 125)
strokeWeight(70)
line(0, -35, 0, -65)  # Body
noStroke()
fill(255)
ellipse(-17.5, -65, 35, 35) # Left eye dome
ellipse(17.5, -65, 35, 35)  # Right eye dome
arc(0, -65, 70, 70, 0, PI)  # Chin
fill(51, 51, 30)
ellipse(-14, -65, 8, 8)     # Left eye
ellipse(14, -65, 8, 8)      # Right eye
quad(0, -58, 4, -51, 0, -44, -4, -51)  # Beak
```

The program grew from 21 lines to 34: the code to draw the first
owl was cut and pasted into the program and a `translate()` was
inserted to move it to the right 70 pixels. This is a tedious and
inefficient way to draw a second owl, not to mention the head-
ache of adding a third owl with this method. But duplicating the
code is unnecessary, because this is the type of situation where
a function can come to the rescue.

Example 9-5: An Owl Function

In this example, a function is introduced to draw two owls with
the same code. If we make the code that draws the owl to the
screen into a new function, the code need only appear once in
the program:

```
def setup():
    size(480, 120)

def draw():
    background(176, 204, 226)
    owl(110, 110)
    owl(180, 110)

def owl(x, y):
    pushMatrix()
    translate(x, y)
    stroke(138, 138, 125)
    strokeWeight(70)
    line(0, -35, 0, -65)    # Body
    noStroke()
    fill(255)
    ellipse(-17.5, -65, 35, 35)    # Left eye dome
    ellipse(17.5, -65, 35, 35)     # Right eye dome
    arc(0, -65, 70, 70, 0, PI)     # Chin
    fill(51, 51, 30)
    ellipse(-14, -65, 8, 8)        # Left eye
    ellipse(14, -65, 8, 8)         # Right eye
    quad(0, -58, 4, -51, 0, -44, -4, -51) # Beak
    popMatrix()
```

You can see from the illustrations that this example and Example 9-4 on page 121 have the same result, but this example is shorter, because the code to draw the owl appears only once, inside the aptly named owl() function. This code runs twice, because it's called twice inside draw(). The owl is drawn in two different locations because of the parameters passed into the function that set the *x* and *y* coordinates.

Parameters are an important part of functions, because they provide flexibility. We saw another example in the rollDice() function; the single parameter named numSides made it possible to simulate a 6-sided die, a 20-sided die, or a die with any number of sides. This is just like many other Processing functions. For instance, the parameters to the line() function make it possible to draw a line from any pixel on screen to any other pixel. Without the parameters, the function would be able to draw a line only from one fixed point to another.

Each parameter is a variable that gets created each time the function runs. When this example is run, the first time the owl function is called, the value of the x parameter is 110, and y is also 110. In the second use of the function, the value of x is 180 and y is again 110. Each value is passed into the function and then wherever the variable name appears within the function, it's replaced with the incoming value.

Example 9-6: Increasing the Surplus Population

Now that we have a basic function to draw the owl at any location, we can draw many owls efficiently by placing the function within a for loop and changing the first parameter each time through the loop:

```
def setup():
    size(480, 120)

def draw():
    background(176, 204, 226)
    for x in range(35, width + 70, 70):
        owl(x, 110)

# Insert owl() function from Example 9-5
```

It's possible to keep adding more and more parameters to the function to change different aspects of how the owl is drawn. Values could be passed in to change the owl's color, rotation, scale, or the diameter of its eyes.

Example 9-7: Owls of Different Sizes

In this example, we've added two parameters to change the gray value and size of each owl:

```
def setup():
  size(480, 120)

def draw():
  background(176, 204, 226)
  randomSeed(0)
  for i in range(35, width + 40, 40):
    gray = int(random(0, 102))
    scalar = random(0.25, 1.0)
    owl(i, 110, gray, scalar)

def owl(x, y, g, s):
  pushMatrix()
  translate(x, y)
  scale(s)  # Set the scale
  stroke(138-g, 138-g, 125-g) # Set the gray value
  strokeWeight(70)
  line(0, -35, 0, -65) # Body
  noStroke()
  fill(255)
  ellipse(-17.5, -65, 35, 35)   # Left eye dome
  ellipse(17.5, -65, 35, 35)    # Right eye dome
  arc(0, -65, 70, 70, 0, PI)    # Chin
  fill(51, 51, 30)
  ellipse(-14, -65, 8, 8) # Left eye
  ellipse(14, -65, 8, 8)  # Right eye
  quad(0, -58, 4, -51, 0, -44, -4, -51) # Beak
  popMatrix()
```

Return Values

Functions can make a calculation and then return a value to the main program. We've already used functions of this type, including `random()` and `sin()`. Notice that when this type of function appears, the return value is usually assigned to a variable:

```
r = random(1, 10)
```

In this case, `random()` returns a value between 1 and 10, which is then assigned to the `r` variable.

A function that returns a value is also frequently used as a parameter to another function. For instance:

```
point(random(width), random(height));
```

In this case, the values from `random()` aren't assigned to a variable—they are passed as parameters to `point()` and used to position the point within the window.

Example 9-8: Return a Value

To make a function that returns a value, specify the data to be passed back with the keyword `return`. For instance, this example includes a function called `calculateMars()` that calculates the weight of a person or object on our neighboring planet:

```
def setup():
    yourWeight = 132.0
    marsWeight = calculateMars(yourWeight)
    print marsWeight

def calculateMars(w):
    newWeight = w * 0.38
    return newWeight
```

Notice the last line of the block, which returns the variable `new Weight`. In the second line of `setup()`, that value is assigned to the variable `marsWeight`. (To see your own weight on Mars, change the value of the `yourWeight` variable to your weight.)

Robot 7: Functions

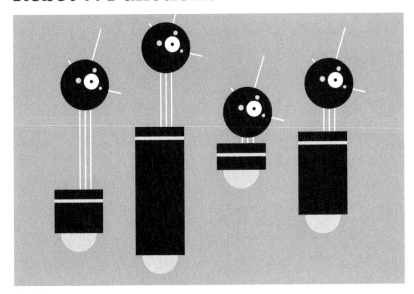

In contrast to Robot 2 (see "Robot 2: Variables" on page 45), this example uses a function to draw four robot variations within the same program. Because the drawRobot() function appears four times within draw(), the code within the drawRobot() block is run four times, each time with a different set of parameters to change the position and height of the robot's body.

Notice how what were global variables in Robot 2 have now been isolated within the drawRobot() function. Because these variables apply only to drawing the robot, they belong inside the drawRobot() function block. Because the value of the radius variable doesn't change, it need not be a parameter. Instead, it is defined at the beginning of drawRobot():

```
def setup():
    size(720, 480)
    strokeWeight(2)
    ellipseMode(RADIUS)

def draw():
    background(0, 153, 204)
    drawRobot(120, 420, 110, 140)
    drawRobot(270, 460, 260, 95)
```

```
drawRobot(420, 310, 80, 10)
drawRobot(570, 390, 180, 40)

def drawRobot(x, y, bodyHeight, neckHeight):

    radius = 45
    ny = y - bodyHeight - neckHeight - radius

    # Neck
    stroke(102)
    line(x+2, y-bodyHeight, x+2, ny)
    line(x+12, y-bodyHeight, x+12, ny)
    line(x+22, y-bodyHeight, x+22, ny)

    # Antennae
    line(x+12, ny, x-18, ny-43)
    line(x+12, ny, x+42, ny-99)
    line(x+12, ny, x+78, ny+15)

    # Body
    noStroke()
    fill(255, 204, 0)
    ellipse(x, y-33, 33, 33)
    fill(0)
    rect(x-45, y-bodyHeight, 90, bodyHeight-33)
    fill(255, 204, 0)
    rect(x-45, y-bodyHeight+17, 90, 6)

    # Head
    fill(0)
    ellipse(x+12, ny, radius, radius)
    fill(255)
    ellipse(x+24, ny-6, 14, 14)
    fill(0)
    ellipse(x+24, ny-6, 3, 3)
    fill(153)
    ellipse(x, ny-8, 5, 5)
    ellipse(x+30, ny-26, 4, 4)
    ellipse(x+41, ny+6, 3, 3)
```

10/Objects

Object-oriented programming (OOP) is a different way to think about your programs. Although the term "object-oriented programming" may sound intimidating, there's good news: you've been working with objects since Chapter 7, when you started using **PImage**, **PFont**, **String**, and **PShape**. Unlike the primitive data types **boolean**, **int**, and **float**, which can store only one value, an object can store many. But that's only a part of the story. Objects are also a way to group variables with related functions. Because you already know how to work with variables and functions, objects simply combine what you've already learned into a more understandable package.

Objects are important, because they break up ideas into smaller building blocks. This mirrors the natural world where, for instance, organs are made of tissue, tissue is made of cells, and so on. Similarly, as your code becomes more complicated, you must think in terms of smaller structures that form more complicated ones. It's easier to write and maintain smaller, understandable pieces of code that work together than it is to write one large piece of code that does everything at once.

Fields and Methods

A software object is a collection of related variables and functions. In the context of objects, a variable is called a *field* (sometimes known as an *instance variable* or *data attribute* in Python) and a function is called a *method*. Fields and methods work in a manner similar to the variables and functions covered in earlier chapters, but we'll use the new terms to emphasize that they are a part of an object. To say it another way, an object combines related data (fields) with related actions and behaviors (methods). The idea is to group together related data with related methods that act on that data.

For instance, to model a radio, think about what parameters can be adjusted and the actions that can affect those parameters:

Fields
> volume, frequency, band(FM, AM), power(on, off)

Methods
> setVolume, setFrequency, setBand

Modeling a simple mechanical device is easy compared to modeling an organism like an ant or a person. It's not possible to reduce such complex organisms to a few fields and methods, but it is possible to model enough to create an interesting simulation. *The Sims* video game is a clear example. This game is played by managing the daily activities of simulated people. The characters have enough personality to make a playable, addictive game, but no more. In fact, they have only five personality attributes: neat, outgoing, active, playful, and nice. With the knowledge that it's possible to make a highly simplified model of complex organisms, we could start programming an ant with only a few fields and methods:

Fields
> type(worker, soldier), weight, length

Methods
> walk, pinch, releasePheromones, eat

If you made a list of an ant's fields and methods, you might choose to focus on different aspects of the ant to model.

There's no right way to make a model, as long as you make it appropriate for the purpose of your program's goals.

Define a Class

Before you can create an object, you must define a class. A *class* is the specification for an object. Using an architectural analogy, a class is like a blueprint for a house, and the object is like the house itself. Each house made from the blueprint can have variations, and the blueprint is only the specification, not a built structure. For example, one house can be blue and another red; one house might come with a fireplace and another without. Likewise with objects, the class defines the data types and behaviors, but each object (house) made from a single class (blueprint) has variables (color, fireplace) that are set to different values. To use a more technical term, each object is an *instance* of a class and each instance has its own set of fields and methods.

Before you write a class, we recommend a little planning. Think about what fields and methods your class should have. Do a little brainstorming to imagine all the possible options and then prioritize and make your best guess about what will work. You'll make changes during the programming process, but it's important to have a good start.

The fields inside a class can be any type of data. A class can simultaneously hold many booleans, floats, images, strings, and so on. Keep in mind that one reason to make a class is to group together related data elements. For your methods, select clear names and decide the return values (if any). The methods are used to change the values of the fields and to perform actions based on the fields' values.

For our first class, we'll convert one of our earlier examples (Example 8-9 on page 106). We start by making a list of the fields from the example:

```
x
y
diameter
speed
```

The next step is to figure out what methods might be useful for the class. In looking at the **draw()** function from the example we're adapting, we see two primary components. The position of the shape is updated and drawn to the screen. Let's create two methods for our class, one for each task:

```
def move()
def display()
```

When we next write the class based on the lists of fields and methods, we'll follow these steps:

1. Write the class definition.
2. Write an __init__ method (explained shortly) to initialize the object and assign values to the fields.
3. Add the methods.

First, we write the class definition:

```
class JitterBug(object):
```

Notice that the keyword **class** is lowercase and the name **Jitter Bug** is uppercase. Naming the class with an uppercase letter isn't required, but it is a convention (that we strongly encourage) used to denote that it's a class. (The keyword **class**, however, must be lowercase because it's a rule of the programming language.)

Second, we add an __init__ method (that's two underscore characters before **init** and two underscore characters after it). Python automatically calls this method whenever an object (an instance of the class) is created. The purpose of the __init__ method is to assign the initial values to the object's fields. You can use the parameters passed to __init__ to initialize fields in the object, or you can initialize fields to a value that doesn't change from one object to the next. For the **JitterBug** class, we've decided that the values for **x**, **y**, and **diameter** will be passed in, but the value for **speed** will be the same for every object that belongs to the class.

The code inside the __init__ method is run once when the object is first created. As discussed earlier, we're passing in three parameters to this method when the object is initialized.

Each of the values passed in is assigned to a temporary variable that exists only while the code inside the __init__ method is run. To clarify this, we've added the name temp to each of these variables, but they can be named with any terms that you prefer. In this example, these variables are used only to assign the values to the fields that are a part of the class. Also note that the __init__ method never returns a value and therefore doesn't have a return statement in it.

After adding the __init__ method, the class looks like this:

```
class JitterBug(object):
    def __init__(self, tempX, tempY, tempDiameter):
        self.x = tempX
        self.y = tempY
        self.diameter = tempDiameter
        self.speed = 0.5
```

The first parameter to any method in Python, including the __init__ method, is the word *self*. This is a special parameter that Python automatically passes to methods. Its value is the object that the method is being called on. The self parameter is what allows you to set the value for a field (e.g., the expression self.x = tempX in the preceding example) or to use the value of that field in an expression.

Figure 10-1 shows another example of a class definition: a "Train" class that has fields for the train's name and distance. The illustration highlights how values flow from the main program to the fields of the newly created object via the __init__ method.

```
class Train(object):

    def __init__(self, tempName, tempDistance):

        self.name = tempName

        self.distance = tempDistance


red = Train("Red Line", 90)  ←────────────    Assign "Red Line" to the name
                                              field for the red object
blue = Train("Blue Line", 120)

                                              Assign 90 to the distance
                                              field for the red object
def setup():

    size(400, 400)
```

```
class Train(object):

    def __init__(self, tempName, tempDistance):

        self.name = tempName

        self.distance = tempDistance


red = Train("Red Line", 90)

blue = Train("Blue Line", 120)  ←────────    Assign "Blue Line" to the name
                                             field for the blue object

def setup():                                 Assign 120 to the distance
                                             field for the blue object
    size(400, 400)
```

Figure 10-1. *Passing values into the __init__ method to set the values for an object's fields*

The last step in creating a class is to add the other methods. This part is straightforward; it's just like writing functions, but here they are contained within the class. Also, note the code spacing. Every line within the class is indented a few spaces to show that it's inside the block. Within the methods, the code is spaced again to clearly show the hierarchy:

```
class JitterBug(object):
    def __init__(self, tempX, tempY, tempDiameter):
        self.x = tempX
        self.y = tempY
        self.diameter = tempDiameter
        self.speed = 0.5

    def move(self):
        self.x += random(-self.speed, self.speed)
        self.y += random(-self.speed, self.speed)

    def display(self):
        ellipse(self.x, self.y, self.diameter, self.diameter)
```

Create Objects

Now that you have defined a class, to use it in a program you must define an object from that class. There are two steps to create an object:

1. Create a variable to store the object.
2. Create (initialize) the object by "calling" the name of the class as though it were a function.

Example 10-1: Make an Object

To make your first object, we'll start by showing how this works within a Processing sketch and then continue by explaining each part in depth:

```
class JitterBug(object):
    def __init__(self, tempX, tempY, tempDiameter):
        self.x = tempX
        self.y = tempY
        self.diameter = tempDiameter
        self.speed = 0.5
```

```
def move(self):
    self.x += random(-self.speed, self.speed)
    self.y += random(-self.speed, self.speed)

def display(self):
    ellipse(self.x, self.y, self.diameter, self.diameter)

bug = JitterBug(240, 60, 20)

def setup():
    size(480, 120)

def draw():
    bug.move()
    bug.display()
```

Once we've created a variable to store the object, the second step is to initialize the object. The syntax for accomplishing this in Python is to write the name of the class that you want to instantiate, followed by a pair of parentheses with parameters inside them. It looks just like you're "calling" the name of the class, as though it were a function:

```
bug = JitterBug(200.0, 250.0, 30)
```

The three numbers within the parentheses are the parameters that are passed into the __init__ method defined in the Jitter Bug class. Because Python automatically inserts self as the first parameter to any method (including __init__), the number of parameters inside the parentheses should be exactly one *fewer* than the number defined in __init__.

Example 10-2: Make Multiple Objects

In Example 10-1 on page 135, we see something else new: the period (dot) that's used to access the object's methods inside of draw(). The dot operator is used to join the name of the object with its fields and methods. This becomes clearer in this example, where two objects are made from the same class. The jit.move() command refers to the move() method that belongs to the object named jit, and bug.move() refers to the move() method that belongs to the object named bug:

```
# Put a copy of the JitterBug class here

jit = JitterBug(160, 60, 50)
bug = JitterBug(320, 60, 10)

def setup():
  size(480, 120)

def draw():
  jit.move()
  jit.display()
  bug.move()
  bug.display()
```

Now that the class exists as its own module of code, any changes will modify the objects made from it. For instance, you could add a field to the JitterBug class that controls the color, or another that determines its size. These values can be passed in using the __init__ method or assigned using additional methods, such as setColor() or setSize(). And because it's a self-contained unit, you can also use the JitterBug class in another sketch.

Code in Tabs

Now is a good time to learn about the tab feature of the Processing Development Environment (Figure 10-2). Tabs allow you to spread your code across more than one file. This makes longer code easier to edit and more manageable in general. A new tab is usually created for each class, which reinforces the modularity of working with classes and makes the code easy to find.

To create a new tab, click on the arrow at the righthand side of the tab bar. When you select New Tab from the menu, you will be prompted to name the tab within the message window. Using

this technique, modify this example's code to try to make a new
tab for the `JitterBug` class.

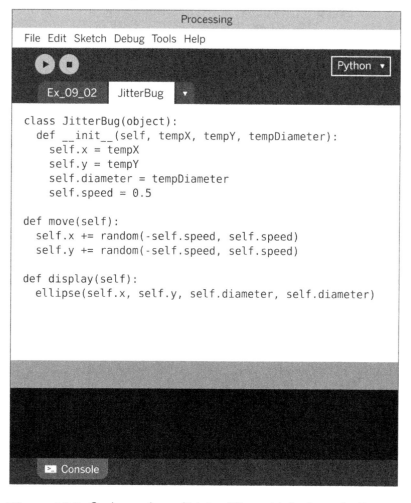

Figure 10-2. *Code can be split into different tabs to make it easier to manage*

Robot 8: Objects

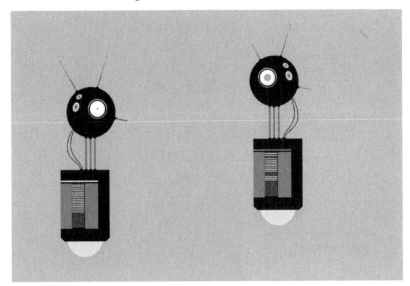

A software object combines methods (functions) and fields (variables) into one unit. The Robot class in this example defines all of the robot objects that will be created from it. Each Robot object has its own set of fields to store a position and the illustration that will draw to the screen. Each has methods to update the position and display the illustration.

The parameters for bot1 and bot2 define the x and y coordinates and the .svg file that will be used to depict the robot. The tempX and tempY parameters are passed into the __init__ method and assigned to the xpos and ypos fields. The svgName parameter is stored in the field svgName, and the file named in the field is loaded later in setup() by calling the loadSvg() method. The objects (bot1 and bot2) draw at their own location and with a different illustration because they each have unique values passed into the objects through their __init__ methods:

```
class Robot(object):
    def __init__(self, tempSvgName, tempX, tempY):
        self.svgName = tempSvgName
        self.xpos = tempX
        self.ypos = tempY
        self.angle = random(0, TWO_PI)
```

```python
      self.yoffset = 0

  def loadSvg(self):
    self.botShape = loadShape(self.svgName)

  def update(self):
    self.angle += 0.05
    self.yoffset = sin(self.angle) * 20

  def display(self):
    shape(self.botShape, self.xpos, self.ypos + self.yoffset);

bot1 = Robot("robot1.svg", 90, 80)
bot2 = Robot("robot2.svg", 440, 30)

def setup():
  size(720, 480)
  bot1.loadSvg()
  bot2.loadSvg()

def draw():
  background(0, 153, 204)

  # Update and display first robot
  bot1.update()
  bot1.display()

  # Update and display second robot
  bot2.update()
  bot2.display()
```

11/Lists

A *list* is a group of variables that share a common name. Lists are useful because they make it possible to work with more variables without creating a new name for each one. This makes the code shorter, easier to read, and more convenient to update.

From Variables to Lists

When a program needs to keep track of one or two things, it's not necessary to use a list. In fact, adding a list might make the program more complicated than necessary. However, when a program has many elements (for example, a field of stars in a space game or multiple data points in a visualization), lists make the code easier to write.

Example 11-1: Many Variables

To see what we mean, refer to Example 8-3 on page 101. This code works fine if we're moving around only one shape, but what if we want to have two? We need to make a new x variable and update it within draw():

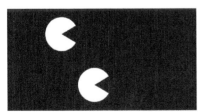 

```
x1 = -20.0
x2 = 20.0

def setup():
  size(240, 120)
  noStroke()

def draw():
  global x1, x2
  background(0)
  x1 += 0.5
  x2 += 0.5
  arc(x1, 30, 40, 40, 0.52, 5.76)
  arc(x2, 90, 40, 40, 0.52, 5.76)
```

Example 11-2: Too Many Variables

The code for the previous example is still manageable, but what if we want to have five circles? We need to add three more variables to the two we already have:

```
x1 = -10.0
x2 = 10.0
x3 = 35.0
x4 = 18.0
x5 = 30.0

def setup():
  size(240, 120)
  noStroke()

def draw():
  global x1, x2, x3, x4, x5
  background(0)
  x1 += 0.5
  x2 += 0.5
  x3 += 0.5
  x4 += 0.5
```

```
x5 += 0.5
arc(x1, 20, 20, 20, 0.52, 5.76)
arc(x2, 40, 20, 20, 0.52, 5.76)
arc(x3, 60, 20, 20, 0.52, 5.76)
arc(x4, 80, 20, 20, 0.52, 5.76)
arc(x5, 100, 20, 20, 0.52, 5.76)
```

This code is starting to get out of control.

Example 11-3: Lists, Not Variables

Imagine what would happen if you wanted to have 3,000 circles. This would mean creating 3,000 individual variables, then updating each one separately. Could you keep track of that many variables? Would you want to? Instead, we use a list:

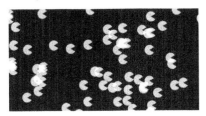

```
x = []

def setup():
  size(240, 120)
  noStroke()
  fill(255, 200)
  for i in range(3000):
    x.append(random(-1000, 200))

def draw():
  background(0)
  for i in range(len(x)):
    x[i] += 0.5
    y = i * 0.4
    arc(x[i], y, 12, 12, 0.52, 5.76)
```

We'll spend the rest of this chapter talking about the details that make this example possible.

List Operations

Each item in a list is called an *element*, and each has an *index* value to mark its position within the list. Just like coordinates on the screen, index values for a list start counting from 0. For instance, the first element in the list has the index value 0, the second element in the list has the index value 1, and so on. If there are 20 values in the list, the index value of the last element is 19. Figure 11-1 shows the conceptual structure of a list.

years = [1920, 1972, 1980, 1996, 2010]

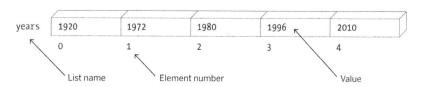

Figure 11-1. *A list is a group of one or more variables that share the same name*

A list value in Python looks like a pair of square brackets. This statement assigns a list to the variable x:

```
x = []
```

You can also initialize the items in the list by putting comma-separated values inside the square brackets:

```
x = [5, 10, 15, 20]
```

Lists in Python can contain values of varying data types. This list has an integer, a floating-point number, and a string:

```
stuff = [89, 1.24, "hello"]
```

You can also use the built-in Python function list() to create a list value:

```
x = list() # creates an empty list
x = list(5, 10, 15, 20) # creates a list with four initial
                        # elements
```

Python list values are objects, and support a number of useful methods. The list method we'll use most is append(), which adds an item to a list:

```
x = [] # x is empty
x.append(5) # now x has one item, the integer value 5
```

Once there are items in your list, you can access the item at a particular index using square bracket syntax. Write the name of the variable that contains your list, followed by a pair of square brackets with a number between them, like so:

```
x = [5, 10, 15, 20]
print x[0] # prints 5
print x[1] # prints 10
print x[2] # prints 15
print x[3] # prints 20
```

List indices in Python are *zero-based*, meaning that the number you use in square brackets to access the first element of the list is 0 (not 1). Likewise, to get the second element, use 1; to get the third element, use 2; and so forth.

After the list has been created, you can *overwrite* the value of an item at a particular index in a list by writing an expression with the square bracket syntax, followed by an equal sign (=) and the new value for that item:

```
x = [5, 10, 15, 20]
print x[2] # prints 15
x[2] = 789
print x[2] # prints 789
```

To determine the length of a list, use Python's built-in `len()` function:

```
x = [5, 10, 15, 20]
print len(x) # prints 4
y = []
print len(y) # prints 0
```

Now that we've looked at some of the basic syntax for working with lists, let's slow down and talk about common ways to use lists in our programs. There are a number of steps to working with a list:

1. Create a list value with square brackets or the `list()` function.

2. Assign that list value to a variable.

3. Optionally, use the list's `append()` method of the list to add new items to the list.

Each of the three following examples shows a different technique to create a list called x that stores two integers, 12 and 2. Pay close attention to what happens before `setup()` and what happens within `setup()`.

Example 11-4: Declare and Append to a List

First, we'll declare an empty list outside of `setup()` and then append values to the list.

```
x = []                  # Create the list

def setup():
  size(200, 200)
  x.append(12)    # Append the first value
  x.append(2)     # Append the second value
```

Example 11-5: Compact List Initialization

Here's a slightly more compact example, in which the list is initialized with its items when the value is first created:

```
x = [12, 2]  # Create a new list with two items, assigned to x

def setup():
  size(200, 200) # No further action needed in setup()!
```

 Avoid creating lists within draw(), because creating a new list on every frame will slow down your frame rate.

Example 11-6: Revisiting the First Example

As a complete example of how to use lists, here we've recoded Example 11-1. Although we don't yet see the full benefits revealed in Example 11-3, we do see some important details of how lists work:

```
x = [-20.0, 20.0]

def setup():
  size(240, 120)
  noStroke()

def draw():
  background(0)
  x[0] += 0.5  # Increase the first element
  x[1] += 0.5  # Increase the second element
  arc(x[0], 30, 40, 40, 0.52, 5.76)
  arc(x[1], 90, 40, 40, 0.52, 5.76)
```

Note that the **global** keyword is not needed in the **draw()** function here. See Appendix D for more information.

Repetition and Lists

The **for** loop, introduced in "Repetition" on page 39, makes it easier to work with large lists while keeping the code concise. The way we use **for** loops to operate on lists is different depending on exactly what we want to do with the list.

Example 11-7: Filling a List in a for Loop

A **for** loop can be used to fill a list with values or to read the values back out. In this example, the list is first filled with random numbers inside **setup()**, and then these numbers are used to set the stroke value inside **draw()**. Each time the program is run, a new set of random numbers is put into the list:

```
gray = []

def setup():
  size(240, 120)
  for i in range(width):
    gray.append(random(0, 255))

def draw():
  for i in range(len(gray)):
    stroke(gray[i])
    line(i, 0, i, height)
```

Example 11-9: Track Mouse Movements

In this example, there are two lists to store the position of the mouse—one for the *x* coordinate and one for the *y* coordinate. These lists store the location of the mouse for every frame. With each new frame, the newest coordinate is inserted at the beginning of the list. This example visualizes this action. Also, at each frame, all coordinates are used to draw a series of ellipses to the screen:

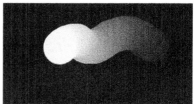

```
x = []
y = []

def setup():
  size(240, 120)
  noStroke()

def draw():
  background(0)
  x.insert(0, mouseX)
  y.insert(0, mouseY)
  for i in range(len(x)):
    fill(i * 4)
    ellipse(x[i], y[i], 40, 40)
```

This example demonstrates another method of the list object, `insert()`, which takes two parameters: the first is an index in the list, and the second is the value to insert into the list at that index. The code `x.insert(0, mouseX)` inserts the value in the variable `mouseX` at index 0 of the list (i.e., the beginning of the list).

 The technique for storing coordinates in a list is inefficient. Because there's no built-in limit to the number of coordinates the list will store, the list in this program can quickly grow very large in memory, causing your sketch to slow down or even crash. For a more efficient technique that only stores the last n numbers, see the Examples → Basics → Input → StoringInput example included with Python Mode.

Lists of Objects

The two short examples in this section bring together every major programming concept in this book: variables, iteration, conditionals, functions, objects, and lists. Making a list of objects is nearly the same as making the lists we introduced on the previous pages, but there's one additional consideration: because each list element is an object, it must first be instantiated before it can be appended to the list. (For a built-in Processing class such as `PImage`, you need to use the `loadImage()` function to create the object before it's assigned.)

Example 11-10: Managing Many Objects

This example creates a list of 33 `JitterBug` objects and then updates and displays each one inside `draw()`. For this example to work, you need to add the `JitterBug` class (see Chapter 10) to the code:

```
# Copy JitterBug class here

bugs = []

def setup():
    size(240, 120)
    for i in range(33):
        x = random(width)
        y = random(height)
        r = i + 2
        bugs.append(JitterBug(x, y, r))

def draw():
    for i in range(len(bugs)):
        bugs[i].move()
        bugs[i].display()
```

Example 11-11: A New Way to Manage Objects

Because iterating over every item in a list is a very common task when writing computer programs, Python has a shorthand syntax for making it easier. Instead of creating a new counter variable, such as the i variable in Example 11-10 on page 149, and iterating over the result of the range() function, it's possible to iterate over the elements of a list directly. In the following example, each object in the bugs list of JitterBug objects is assigned to b in order to run the move() and display() methods for all objects in the list.

This form of the for loop is often tidier than looping with a number, although in this example, we didn't use it inside setup() because i was needed inside the loop (to set the size of the JitterBug object). This demonstrates how it's sometimes helpful to have the number around:

```
# Copy JitterBug class here

bugs = []

def setup():
  size(240, 120)
  for i in range(33):
    x = random(width)
    y = random(height)
    r = i + 2
    bugs.append(JitterBug(x, y, r))

def draw():
  for b in bugs:
    b.move()
    b.display()
```

The final list example loads a sequence of images and stores each as an element within a list of PImage objects.

Example 11-12: Sequences of Images

To run this example, get the images from the *media.zip* file as described in Chapter 7. The images are named sequentially (*frame-0000.png*, *frame-0001.png*, etc.), which makes it possible to create the name of each file within a for loop, as seen in the eighth line of the program:

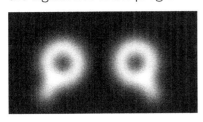

```
numFrames = 12   # The number of frames
images = []      # Make the list
currentFrame = 0

def setup():
  size(240, 120)
  for i in range(numFrames):
    imageName = "frame-" + nf(i, 4) + ".png"
    images.append(loadImage(imageName))
  frameRate(24)
```

```
def draw():
    global currentFrame
    image(images[currentFrame], 0, 0)
    currentFrame += 1   # Next frame
    if currentFrame >= len(images):
        currentFrame = 0  # Return to first frame
```

The nf() function formats numbers so that nf(1, 4) returns the string "0001" and nf(11, 4) returns "0011". These values are concatenated with the beginning of the filename ("frame-") and the end (".png") to create the complete filename as a string. The files are appended to the list on the following line. The images are displayed to the screen one at a time in draw(). When the last image in the list is displayed, the program returns to the beginning of the list and shows the images again in sequence.

Robot 9: Lists

Lists make it easier for a program to work with many elements. In this example, a list intended to contain Robot objects is created at the top. The list is then filled with Robot objects inside setup(). In draw(), another for loop is used to update and display each element of the bots list.

The **for** loop and a list make a powerful combination. Notice the subtle differences between the code for this example and Robot 8 (see "Robot 8: Objects" on page 139) in contrast to the extreme changes in the visual result. Once a list is created and a **for** loop is put in place, it's as easy to work with three elements as it is 3,000.

The decision to load the SVG file within **setup()** rather than in the **Robot** class is the major change from Robot 8. This choice was made so the file is loaded only once, rather than as many times as there are elements in the list (in this case, 20 times). This change makes the code start faster because loading a file takes time, and it uses less memory because the file is stored once. Each element of the **bot** list references the same file:

```
class Robot(object):

    # Set initial values
    def __init__(self, shape, tempX, tempY):
        self.botShape = shape
        self.xpos = tempX
        self.ypos = tempY
        self.angle = random(0, TWO_PI)
        self.yoffset = 0.0

    def update(self):
        self.angle += 0.05
        self.yoffset = sin(self.angle) * 20

    def display(self):
        shape(self.botShape, self.xpos, self.ypos + self.yoffset)


bots = []   # Create list for Robot objects
botCount = 20

def setup():
    size(720, 480)
    robotShape = loadShape("robot1.svg")
    # Create each object
    for i in range(botCount):
        # Create a random x coordinate
        x = random(-40, width-40)
        # Assign the y coordinate based on the order
        y = map(i, 0, botCount, -100, height-200)
```

```
      bots.append(Robot(robotShape, x, y))

def draw():
  background(0, 153, 204)
  for b in bots:
    b.update()
    b.display()
```

12/Data and Dictionaries

Data visualization is one of the most active areas at the intersection of code and graphics and is also one of the most popular uses of Processing. This chapter builds on what has been discussed about storing and loading data earlier in the book and introduces more features relevant to data sets that might be used for visualization.

There is a wide range of software that can output standard visualizations like bar charts and scatter plots. However, writing code to create visualization from scratch provides more control over the output and encourages users to imagine, explore, and create more unique representations of data. For us, this is the point of learning to code and using software like Processing, and we find it far more interesting than being limited by prepackaged methods or tools that are available.

Data Summary

It's a good time to rewind and discuss how data was introduced throughout this book. Recall that every value in a Python program has a *data type*. Each kind of data is unique and is stored in a different way. We started the book talking about simple data types like *int* (for integers) or *float* (for numbers with decimals). Later, we discussed *compound data types* like objects and lists. A compound data type keeps track of multiple values. The values in a list are accessed by their numerical index, whereas the values in an object are accessed by name as data attributes.

The examples in this chapter introduce a new compound data type: the *dictionary*. Dictionaries are data structures that are conceptually similar to lists, except instead of accessing values by numerical index, you access them by name. This makes dictionaries a data type especially suited for storing, transmitting, and processing structured data. There are several built-in Python tools that read data in various formats (e.g., from the *data* folder for a sketch) and return dictionaries. We'll load data into dictionaries from two different sources: tables of data in comma-separated values (CSV) format, and data in JSON format.

Dictionaries

You can think of a dictionary as being sort of like a list, except you index its values not with a number but with a *key*. Dictionary keys are usually strings that identify the values they point to in an easy-to-remember way. Let's say, for example, that we wanted to include in our sketch some information about the planets of our solar system. Here's what a dictionary with information about Earth might look like in Python:

```
planetInfo = {
    "name": "Earth",
    "knownMoons": 1,
    "eqRadiusKm": 6387.1,
    "hasRings": False
}
```

In this example, we've created a dictionary and assigned it to a variable called `planetInfo`. The *keys* in this dictionary are `name`, `knownMoons`, `eqRadiusKm`, and `hasRings`. The values for those keys are `Earth`, `1`, `6387.1`, and `False`, respectively. As this example shows, dictionary values can be any data type: strings, integers, floating-point numbers, booleans—even objects, lists, and other dictionaries can be stored as dictionary values.

Once you've defined a dictionary, you can get the value for a particular key using square bracket notation. This looks similar to how you get the value for a particular index in a list, except this time we're putting a string between the square brackets instead of a number:

```
planetInfo = {
  "name": "Earth",
  "knownMoons": 1,
  "eqRadiusKm": 6387.1,
  "hasRings": False
}
print planetInfo['name'] # prints "Earth"
print planetInfo['knownMoons'] # prints 1
```

If you attempt to get the value for a key that is not present in the dictionary, Python will raise a KeyError, and your program will halt:

```
print planetInfo['extraterrestrialCount'] # raises KeyError
```

You can check to see whether or not a key is present in a dictionary by using the special operator in. Put the key you want to check for on the lefthand side of in, and the dictionary you want to check on the righthand side. The entire expression will return True or False, so you can use it in an if statement:

```
print 'extraterrestrialCount' in planetInfo # prints False
if 'eqRadiusKm' in planetInfo:
  print "Planetary radius (km): ", planetInfo['eqRadiusKm']
else:
  print "No radius information available."
```

The name *dictionary* is meant to evoke a physical dictionary, in which you look up words (*keys*) to find their definitions (*values*). In other computer languages (such as Java and C++), the analogous data structure is called a *map*. Sometimes when talking about dictionaries, we'll say that keys "map" to values. (For instance, in the preceding example, the key name maps to the value Earth.)

Example 12-1: (Keyboard) Keys as (Dictionary) Keys

The following sketch shows how dictionaries can be used to store information and retrieve it in response to user input:

```
sizes = {
    'a': 40,
    'b': 80,
    'c': 120,
    'd': 160
}
def setup():
    size(200, 200)
    rectMode(CENTER)
def draw():
    background(0)
    fill(255)
    if keyPressed:
        if key in sizes:
            rect(100, 100, sizes[key], sizes[key])
```

This sketch displays rectangles of various sizes to the screen in response to user input. A dictionary called `sizes` maps particular keystrokes to integer values. Inside of `draw()`, we check to see if a keyboard key has been pressed and whether the string value of that keyboard key is present in the `sizes` dictionary. If so, we display a rectangle with its size determined by the value stored for that key.

Lists of Dictionaries

Let's return to our dictionary with information about a particular planet. It looks like this:

```
planetInfo = {
    "name": "Earth",
    "knownMoons": 1,
    "eqRadiusKm": 6387.1,
    "hasRings": False
}
```

Now, let's imagine that we want our program to contain information not just about Earth, but all of the terrestrial planets

(Mercury, Venus, Earth, and Mars). We could do this by creating several dictionaries, one for each planet:

```
mercuryInfo = {
    "name": "Mercury",
    "knownMoons": 0,
    "eqRadiusKm": 2439.64,
}
venusInfo = {
    "name": "Venus",
    "knownMoons": 0,
    "eqRadiusKm": 6051.59,
}
earthInfo = {
    "name": "Earth",
    "knownMoons": 1,
    "eqRadiusKm": 6387.1,
}
marsInfo = {
    "name": "Mars",
    "knownMoons": 2,
    "eqRadiusKm": 3397.0
}
```

So far, so good. Let's set ourselves to another task: how would you calculate the *average equatorial radius* for all planets in this data? Here's the most obvious way to do it:

```
planetCount = 4
radiusSum = mercuryInfo['eqRadiusKm']
radiusSum += venusInfo['eqRadiusKm']
radiusSum += earthInfo['eqRadiusKm']
radiusSum += marsInfo['eqRadiusKm']
print radiusSum / planetCount # prints 4568.8325
```

But this solution has some problems, the foremost being the repetition. If we add more planet data, we would have to manually add each new planet to our statements that calculate the sum of their radii. This could get tedious very quickly.

Thankfully, in just the same way that Python allows us to make lists of integers or floating-point numbers, we can create *lists of dictionaries*:

```
planetList = [mercuryInfo, venusInfo, earthInfo, marsInfo]
```

This statement creates a list called `planetList`. Each element of `planetList` is a dictionary. We can access any value for a particular key for one of the dictionaries in this list like so:

```
print planetList[2]['name'] # prints 'Earth'
print planetList[3]['knownMoons'] # prints 2
```

That's a lot of square brackets! Here's how to understand what an expression like `planetList[2]['name']` means. First, we know that we can put square brackets with a number inside (e.g., `[2]`) right after any expression that evaluates to a list. That expression will evaluate to the value stored at that index of the list, which in this case is a dictionary. We also know that we can put square brackets with a string inside (e.g., `['name']`) right after any expression that evaluates to a dictionary. That expression will, in turn, evaluate to the value stored in the dictionary for that key. Keeping both of these ways to form expressions in mind, you can read the expression `planetList[2]['name']` from left to right like so:

- `planetList` is a list
- `planetList[2]` is the element at index 2 of `planetList`, which is a dictionary
- `planetList[2]['name']` is the value for key name in that dictionary (`Earth`)

We can loop over a list of dictionaries the same way we loop over a regular list, with a **for** loop:

```
radiusSum = 0
for i in range(len(planetList)):
    radiusSum += planetList[i]['eqRadiusKm']
print radiusSum / len(planetList) # prints 4568.8325
```

Alternatively, we can use the **for...in** looping syntax introduced in Example 11-11 on page 150. The "temporary loop variable" in this case will be a dictionary. With that in mind, here's some revised code to calculate the average radius of all four terrestrial planets:

```
radiusSum = 0
for p in planetList:
    radiusSum += p['eqRadiusKm']
print radiusSum / len(planetList) # prints 4568.8325
```

Example 12-2: The Planets

This example takes a simplified version of our list of planet information dictionaries and uses it as a data source for drawing to the screen:

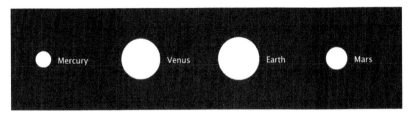

```
planetList = [
  {"name": "Mercury", "eqRadiusKm": 2439.64},
  {"name": "Venus", "eqRadiusKm": 6051.59},
  {"name": "Earth", "eqRadiusKm": 6387.1},
  {"name": "Mars", "eqRadiusKm": 3397.0}
]
def setup():
  size(600, 150)
  textAlign(LEFT, CENTER)
def draw():
  background(0)
  fill(255)
  planetCount = len(planetList)
  for i in range(planetCount):
    # scale radius to be screen-friendly
    planetRadius = planetList[i]['eqRadiusKm'] * 0.01
    offset = 50 + ((width/planetCount) * i)
    ellipse(offset, height/2, planetRadius, planetRadius)
    text(planetList[i]['name'], 10+offset+(planetRadius/2),
      height/2)
```

The sketch begins with a simplified version of our planet
List variable. Here, instead of creating a variable for each dictionary first and then putting the variable names into the list declaration, we simply write the dictionaries straight into the list. In the draw() function, we loop over the list of planets and use each planet's radius and name to draw it to the screen (using the planet's position in the list to determine where on the screen to draw it).

CSV Files

Many data sets are stored in spreadsheets. You may have worked with a program like Microsoft Excel or Google Sheets that allows you to manipulate data in this format. Spreadsheets are made out of rows and columns, with each row usually representing one item and each cell in the row representing some aspect of that item.

Spreadsheet data is often stored in plain-text files with columns using commas or the tab character. A *comma-separated values* file is abbreviated as *CSV*, and uses the file extension *.csv*. When tabs are used, the extension *.tsv* is sometimes used. Python includes a library to make it easy to work with data stored in this format. In this chapter, we will focus on loading data from a CSV file.

To load a CSV or TSV file, you'll need to place it in your sketch's *data* folder (as described in Chapter 7).

The data for the next example is a simplified version of Boston Red Sox player David Ortiz's batting statistics from 1997 to 2014. From left to right, it is the year, number of home runs, runs batted in (RBIs), and batting average. When opened in a text editor, the first five lines of the file look like this:

```
1997,1,6,0.327
1998,9,46,0.277
1999,0,0,0
2000,10,63,0.282
2001,18,48,0.234
```

Example 12-3: Read the Data

To load this data into Processing, we need to use one of Python's built-in libraries called *csv*. The *csv* library provides functions and classes that make it easy to work with data in CSV format. We also need to use the built-in Python function `open()` to gain access to the file in the sketch's data folder. Once we've created a CSV reader object, we use a `for` loop to operate on each row of data in sequence:

```
import csv

statsFileHandle = open("ortiz.csv")
statsData = csv.reader(statsFileHandle)
for row in statsData:
  year = row[0]
  homeRuns = row[1]
  rbi = row[2]
  average = row[3]
  print year, homeRuns, rbi, average
```

The **import** statement at the beginning of the program is what signals to Python that we want to use the built-in *csv* library in our program. The **open()** function takes the name of the CSV file we want to work with as a parameter, and returns a special kind of object called a *file handle*. We then pass that file handle as a parameter to the **csv.reader()** function, which returns a CSV reader object (which we've assigned to a variable called *statsData* here). A CSV reader object works a lot like a list, in that we can iterate over it with a **for** loop. (We've called the temporary loop variable here **row**, but there's nothing special about that word. You can call it whatever you want!)

Inside the **for** loop, we can access data for the current row using the numerical index of the relevant column. The expression **row[0]** evaluates to the item in the first column of the row (i.e., the year), the expression **row[1]** evaluates to the item in the second column, and so forth.

Getting the Right Type

There's one tricky thing about using CSV files, which is that they don't contain any information about what *kind* of data they're storing. To illustrate, think about how you might go about finding the sum of David Ortiz's home runs in his career. You might write some code that looks like this:

```
import csv

statsFileHandle = open("ortiz.csv")
statsData = csv.reader(statsFileHandle)

homeRunTotal = 0
for row in statsData:
```

```
    homeRunTotal += row[1]

  print homeRunTotal
```

In this code, we made a variable called homeRunTotal to store the total number of home runs. As we iterate over each row, we add the number from the second column, which contains the number of home runs for that year. Looks good, right? But there's a problem. If you try to run this, you'll get the following error:

```
TypeError: unsupported operand type(s) for +: 'int' and 'str'
```

This error is telling you that you were attempting to add an int to a str. Python doesn't know how to do that, so your program didn't work. This happened because the *csv* library always gives you data from a CSV file as a *string*, even if the underlying data *looks* like a number. If you want to use that string as a number, you have to explicitly convert it yourself, using one of Python's built-in conversion functions like int().

Here's a corrected version of the preceding example. The only change we've made is to the line inside the for loop, where we use the int() function to convert the value from the CSV file from a string to an int:

```
import csv

statsFileHandle = open("ortiz.csv")
statsData = csv.reader(statsFileHandle)

homeRunTotal = 0
for row in statsData:
  homeRunTotal += int(row[1])

print homeRunTotal
```

Example 12-4: Draw the Table

The next example builds on the last. It creates a list called homeRuns to store data after it is loaded inside setup() and the data from that list is used within draw(). In setup(), we again use open() to get a file handle for our CSV file, and then give the file handle as a parameter to csv.reader(). In a for loop, we append each home run count to our **homeRuns** list, taking care to convert the values to integers first.

Two separate tasks are accomplished in **draw()**. First, a **for** loop draws vertical lines for our graph based on the number of entries in the **homeRuns** list. A second **for** loop reads each element of the **homeRuns** list and plots a line on the graph using the data.

This example is the visualization of a simplified version of Boston Red Sox player David Ortiz's batting statistics from 1997 to 2014 drawn from a table:

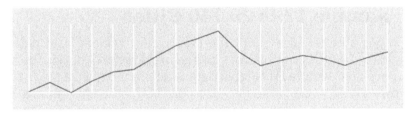

```
import csv

homeRuns = list()

def setup():
    size(480, 120)
    statsFileHandle = open("ortiz.csv")
    statsData = csv.reader(statsFileHandle)
    for row in statsData:
        homeRuns.append(int(row[1]))
    print homeRuns

def draw():
    background(204)
    # Draw background grid for data
    stroke(153)
    line(20, 100, 20, 20)
    line(20, 100, 460, 100)
    for i in range(len(homeRuns)):
        x = map(i, 0, len(homeRuns)-1, 20, 460)
        line(x, 20, x, 100)
    # Draw lines based on home run data
    noFill()
    stroke(0)
    beginShape()
```

```
for i in range(len(homeRuns)):
    x = map(i, 0, len(homeRuns)-1, 20, 460)
    y = map(homeRuns[i], 0, 60, 100, 20)
    vertex(x, y)
endShape()
```

This example is so minimal that it's not necessary to store this data in lists, but the idea can be applied to more complex examples you might want to make in the future. In addition, you can see how this example will be enhanced with more information—for instance, information on the vertical axis to state the number of home runs and on the horizontal to define the year.

Example 12-5: 29,740 Cities

To get a better idea about the potential of working with data tables, the next example uses a larger data set and introduces a convenient feature. This table data is different because the first row—the first line in the file—is a *header*. The header defines a label for each column to clarify the context. This is the first five lines of our new data file called *cities.csv*:

```
zip,state,city,lat,lng
35004,AL,Acmar,33.584132,-86.51557
35005,AL,Adamsville,33.588437,-86.959727
35006,AL,Adger,33.434277,-87.167455
35007,AL,Keystone,33.236868,-86.812861
```

The header makes it easier to read the data—for example, the second line of the file states the zip code of Acmar, Alabama, is 35004 and defines the latitude of the city as 33.584132 and the longitude as -86.51557. In total, the file is 29,741 lines long and it defines the location and zip codes of 29,740 cities in the United States.

The next example loads this data within the `setup()` and then draws it to the screen in a `for` loop within the `draw()`. The `setXY()` function converts the latitude and longitude data from the file into a point on the screen:

```
import csv

citiesData = None

def setXY(lat, lng):
  x = map(lng, -180, 180, 0, width)
  y = map(lat, 90, -90, 0, height)
  point(x, y)

def setup():
  global citiesData
  size(240, 120)
  citiesFileHandle = open("cities.csv")
  citiesData = list(csv.DictReader(citiesFileHandle))
  strokeWeight(0.1)
  stroke(255)

def draw():
  background(0, 26, 51)
  xoffset = map(mouseX, 0, width, -width*3, -width)
  translate(xoffset, -300)
  scale(10)
  for row in citiesData:
    latitude = float(row["lat"])
    longitude = float(row["lng"])
    setXY(latitude, longitude)
```

The csv.DictReader object is a little different from the csv.reader object that we used in the previous example. When we used the csv.reader object, we had to access each cell in a row of data by its numerical index. The csv.DictReader object, on the other hand, gives us a *dictionary* for each row. This dictionary uses the strings in the header line of the CSV file as its keys, and each key maps to the corresponding value for the row in question. Because each row is a dictionary, we can use (for example) the expression row["lat"] to access the latitude column, which is much easier to remember than if we needed to reference the column by its numerical index.

You may have noticed the curious use of the built-in `list()` function in `setup()`. This is necessary because `csv.DictReader` objects, unlike regular lists, can only be iterated over once. We use the `list()` function to read all of the rows from one of these objects at once and store them in a separate variable. The resulting value, stored in the variable `citiesData`, is a list of dictionaries (much like the `planetsList` variable in Example 12-2 on page 161).

JSON

The JavaScript Object Notation (JSON) format is another common system for storing data. Like HTML and XML formats, the elements have labels associated with them. For instance, the data for a film might include labels for the title, director, release year, rating, and more. These labels will be paired with the data like this:

```
"title": "Alphaville"
"director": "Jean-Luc Godard"
"year": 1964
"rating": 9.1
```

To work as a JSON file, the film labels need a little more punctuation to separate the elements. Commas are used between each data pair, and braces enclose it. The data defined within the curly braces is a *JSON object*.

With these changes, our valid JSON data file looks like this:

```
{
  "title": "Alphaville",
  "director": "Jean-Luc Godard",
  "year": 1964,
  "rating": 9.1
}
```

There's another interesting detail in this short JSON sample related to data types: you'll notice that the title and director data is contained within quotes to mark them as strings, and the year and rating are without quotes to define them as numbers. Specifically, the year is an integer and the rating is a floating-point number. This distinction becomes important after the data is loaded into a sketch.

To add another film to the list, a set of brackets placed at the top and bottom are used to signify that the data is an array of JSON objects. Each object is separated by a comma.

Putting it together looks like this:

```
[
  {
    "title": "Alphaville",
    "director": "Jean-Luc Godard",
    "year": 1964,
    "rating": 9.1
  },
  {
    "title": "Pierrot le fou",
    "director": "Jean-Luc Godard",
    "year": 1965,
    "rating": 7.3
  }
]
```

This pattern can be repeated to include more films. At this point, it's interesting to compare this JSON notation to the corresponding CSV representation of the same data.

As a CSV file, the data looks like this:

```
title,director,year,rating
Alphaville,Jean-Luc Godard,1965,9.1
Weekend,Jean-Luc Godard,1967,7.3
```

Notice that the CSV notation has fewer characters, which can be important when working with massive data sets. On the other hand, the JSON version is often easier to read because each piece of data is labeled.

Now that the basics of JSON and its relation to CSV data has been introduced, let's look at the code needed to read a JSON file into a Processing sketch.

Example 12-6: Read a JSON File

You may have noticed that the JSON format looks very similar to the way Python data structures look when we include them directly in our program. This similarity is a little misleading, as there are a number of subtle differences between the two, and you can't just paste a JSON data structure verbatim into your Python program and expect it to work. What we need is a way to read data stored in JSON format and convert it into a Python data structure that we can use in our program. Python supplies us with this functionality through the built-in *json* library.

This sketch loads the JSON file from the beginning of this section, the file that includes only the data for the film *Alphaville*:

```python
import json

def setup():
    filmFileHandle = open("film.json")
    film = json.load(filmFileHandle)
    title = film["title"]
    director = film["director"]
    year = film["year"]
    rating = film["rating"]
    print "Title: ", title
    print "Director: ", director
    print "Year: ", year
    print "Rating: ", rating
```

The `json.load()` function loads data in JSON format from a given file handle. (Just as with the CSV examples, we need to create the file handle first with the built-in `open()` function.) The `json.load()` function returns a value of a compound data type that corresponds to the data in the JSON file. In this example, the JSON object in *film.json* is converted into a Python dictionary, which we store in the variable `film`. We can then use square bracket syntax to access values for particular keys in that dictionary. After we've converted the JSON into Python, the types of the values retrieved will reflect their types from the original JSON data structure (i.e., JSON integers will become Python integers, JSON strings will become Python strings, etc.).

Example 12-7: Visualize Data from a JSON File

In this example, the data file started before has been updated to include all of the director's films from 1960–1966. The name of each film is placed in order on screen according to the release year and assigned a gray value based on the rating value.

There are several differences between this example and Example 12-4 on page 164. The most important is the fact that the data structure in *films.json* is a list of dictionaries, not just a single dictionary. As a result, the call to json.load() in setup() returns a list. Each item in this list is a dictionary that contains data for a particular film. Inside draw(), we iterate over each item in this list and display its values to the screen:

```
import json

films = []

def setup():
    global films
    size(480, 120)
    filmFileHandle = open("films.json")
    films = json.load(filmFileHandle)

def draw():
    background(0)
    for i in range(len(films)):
        film = films[i]
        ratingGray = map(film["rating"], 6.5, 8.1, 102, 255)
        pushMatrix()
        translate(i*32 + 32, 105)
        rotate(-QUARTER_PI)
        fill(ratingGray)
        text(film["title"], 0, 0)
        popMatrix()
```

This example is bare bones in its visualization of the film data. It shows how to load the data and how to draw based on those data values, but it's your challenge to format it to accentuate what you find interesting about the data. For example, is it more interesting to show the number of films Godard made each year? Is it more interesting to compare and contrast this data with the films of another director? Will all of this be easier to read with a different font, sketch size, or aspect ratio? The skills introduced in the earlier chapters in this book can be applied to bring this sketch to the next step of refinement.

Network Data and APIs

Public access to massive quantities of data collected by governments, corporations, organizations, and individuals is changing our culture, from the way we socialize to how we think about intangible ideas like privacy. This data is most often accessed through software structures called *APIs*.

The acronym *API* is mysterious, and its meaning—application programming interface—isn't much clearer. However, APIs are essential for working with data and they aren't necessarily difficult to understand. Essentially, they are requests for data made to a service. When data sets are huge, it's not practical or desired to copy the entirety of the data; an API allows a programmer to request only the trickle of data that is relevant from a massive sea.

This concept can be more clearly illustrated with a hypothetical example. Let's assume there's an organization that maintains a database of temperature ranges for every city within a country. The API for this dataset allows a programmer to request the high and low temperatures for any city during the month of October in 1972. In order to access this data, the request must be made through a specific line or lines of code, in the format mandated by the data service.

Some APIs are entirely public, but many require authentication, which is typically a unique user ID or key so the data service can keep track of its users. Most APIs have rules about how many, or how frequently, requests can be made. For instance, it might be possible to make only 1,000 requests per month, or no more than one request per second. Many APIs also require you to register as a developer on their site to obtain an "API key," a special identifying string that must be included with the API request.

Processing can request data over the Internet when the computer that is running the program is online. CSV, TSV, JSON, and XML files can be loaded using the corresponding load function with a URL as the parameter. For instance, the current weather in Cincinnati is available in JSON format at this URL:

- *http://api.openweathermap.org/data/2.5/find?q=Cincinnati&units=imperial&appid=YOUR_API_KEY*

Read the URL closely to decode it:

1. It requests data from the *api* subdomain of the *openweathermap.org* site.
2. It specifies a city to search for (*q* is an abbreviation for *query*, and is frequently used in URLs that specify searches).
3. It indicates that the data will be returned in imperial format, which means the temperature will be in Fahrenheit. Replacing *imperial* with *metric* will provide temperature data in degrees Celsius.
4. It includes your API key, supplied as the `appid` parameter.

Visit *http://openweathermap.org/api* for more information on accessing the Open Weather Map API and obtaining an API key.

Looking at this data from OpenWeatherMap is a more realistic example of working with data found in the wild rather than the simplified data sets introduced earlier. At the time of this writing, the file returned from that URL looks like this:

```
{"message":"accurate","cod":"200","count":1,"list":[{"id":
4508722,"name":"Cincinnati","coord":{"lon":-84.456886,"lat":
39.161999},"main":{"temp":34.16,"temp_min":34.16,"temp_max":
34.16,"pressure":999.98,"sea_level":1028.34,"grnd_level":
999.98,"humidity":77},"dt":1423501526,"wind":{"speed":
9.48,"deg":354.002},"sys":{"country":"US"},"clouds":{"all":
80},"weather":[{"id":803,"main":"Clouds","description":"broken
clouds","icon":"04d"}]}]}
```

This file is much easier to read when it's formatted with line breaks and the JSON object and list structures defined with braces and brackets:

```
{
  "message": "accurate",
  "count": 1,
  "cod": "200",
  "list": [{
    "clouds": {"all": 80},
    "dt": 1423501526,
    "coord": {
      "lon": -84.456886,
      "lat": 39.161999
    },
    "id": 4508722,
    "wind": {
      "speed": 9.48,
      "deg": 354.002
    },
    "sys": {"country": "US"},
    "name": "Cincinnati",
    "weather": [{
      "id": 803,
      "icon": "04d",
      "description": "broken clouds",
      "main": "Clouds"
    }],
    "main": {
      "humidity": 77,
      "pressure": 999.98,
      "temp_max": 34.16,
      "sea_level": 1028.34,
      "temp_min": 34.16,
      "temp": 34.16,
      "grnd_level": 999.98
    }
  }]
}
```

Note that brackets are seen in the `"list"` and `"weather"` sections, indicating a list of JSON objects. Although the list in this example only contains a single item, in other cases, the API might return multiple days or variations of the data from multiple weather stations.

Example 12-8: Parsing the Weather Data

The first step in working with this data is to study it and then to write minimal code to extract the desired data. In this case, we're curious about the current temperature. We can see that our temperature data is 34.16. It's labeled as `temp` and it's inside the `main` object, which is inside the list of objects given as a value for the key `list`. A function called `getTemp()` was written for this example to work with the format of this specific JSON file organization:

```python
import json

def getTemp(fileName):
    weatherFileHandle = open(fileName)
    weather = json.load(weatherFileHandle)
    list_value = weather["list"] # get value for "list" key
    item = list_value[0] # get first item from list_value
    main = item["main"] # item is a dictionary; get "main" value
    temperature = main["temp"] # get value for "temp" key
    return temperature

def setup():
    temp = getTemp("cincinnati.json")
    print temp
```

The name of the JSON file, *cincinnati.json*, is passed into the `getTemp()` function inside `setup()` and loaded there. Next, because of the format of the JSON file, a series of lists and dictionaries are needed to get deeper and deeper into the data structure to finally arrive at our desired number. This number is stored in the `temperature` variable and then returned by the function to be assigned to the `temp` variable in `setup()` where it is printed to the console.

Example 12-9: Chaining Square Brackets

The sequence of JSON variables created in succession in the last example can be approached differently by chaining the indexes together. This example works like Example 12-8 on page 175 except that each square bracket index is connected directly to the previous one, rather than calculated one at a time and assigned to variables in between:

```python
import json

def getTemp(fileName):
    weather = json.load(open(fileName))
    return weather["list"][0]["main"]["temp"]

def setup():
    temp = getTemp("cincinnati.json")
    print temp
```

This example can be modified to access more of the data from the feed and to build a sketch that displays the data to the screen rather than just writing it to the console. You can also modify it to read data from another online API—you'll find that the data returned by many APIs shares a similar format.

Robot 10: Data

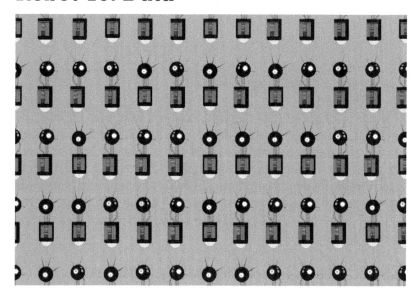

The final robot example in this book is different from the rest because it has two parts. The first part generates a data file using random values and **for** loops, and the second part reads that data file to draw an army of robots onto the screen.

The first sketch uses several new code elements. First, we'll use the open() function to create a new file, and then we'll use the file handle object's write() method to write data to that file. In this example, the file handle object is called output and the file is called *botArmy.tsv*. (You'll need to adjust the path in the following example to reflect a folder that exists on your own computer.) Random values are used to define which of three robot images will be drawn for each coordinate. For the file to be correctly created, the close() method must be run before the program is stopped.

Notice that we called the open() function in this example with a second parameter: the string "w". This parameter signals to Python that we want to open the file not just to read its contents, but to write new contents to it. (The *w* stands for *write*.)

The code that draws an ellipse is a visual preview to reveal the location of the coordinate on screen, but notice that the ellipse isn't recorded into the file. Also note that the we need to use the str() function to explicitly convert the x, y, and robotType values to strings so that we can build the line of text that gets written to the file:

```
def setup():
    size(720, 480)
    # Create the new file
    output = open("/Users/allison/botArmy.tsv", "w")
    # Write a header line with the column titles
    output.write("type\tx\ty\n")
    for y in range(0, height+1, 60):
        for x in range(0, width+1, 20):
            robotType = str(int(random(1, 4)))
            output.write(robotType+"\t"+str(x)+"\t"+str(y)+"\n")
            ellipse(x, y, 12, 12)
    output.close()  # Finish the file
```

After that program is run, you'll find a file named *botArmy.tsv* in the location you specified in the first parameter to the open() function. Open it to see how the data is written. The first five lines of that file will be similar to this:

type	x	y
3	0	0
1	20	0
2	40	0

```
1     60     0
3     80     0
```

The first column is used to define which robot image to use, the second column is the *x* coordinate, and the third column is the *y* coordinate.

The next sketch loads the *botArmy.tsv* file and uses the data for these purposes. Note that because the data was written in tab-separated values (TSV) format instead of comma-separated values (CSV) format, we need to include `delimiter="\t"` as an extra parameter in the call to *csv.DictReader*:

```python
import csv

def setup():
    size(720, 480)
    background(0, 153, 204)
    bot1 = loadShape("robot1.svg")
    bot2 = loadShape("robot2.svg")
    bot3 = loadShape("robot3.svg")
    shapeMode(CENTER)
    robotsFileHandle = open("/Users/allison/botArmy.tsv")
    robots = csv.DictReader(robotsFileHandle, delimiter="\t")
    for row in robots:
        bot = int(row["type"])
        x = int(row["x"])
        y = int(row["y"])
        sc = 0.3
        if bot == 1:
            shape(bot1, x, y, bot1.width*sc, bot1.height*sc)
        elif bot == 2:
            shape(bot2, x, y, bot2.width*sc, bot2.height*sc)
        else:
            shape(bot3, x, y, bot3.width*sc, bot3.height*sc)
```

13/Extend

This book focuses on using Processing for interactive graphics, because that's the core of what Processing does. However, the software can do much more and is often part of projects that move beyond a single computer screen. For example, Processing has been used to control machines, create images used in feature films, and export models for 3D printing.

Over the last decade, Processing has been used to make music videos for Radiohead and R.E.M., to make illustrations for publications such as *Nature* and the *New York Times*, to output sculptures for gallery exhibitions, to control huge video walls, to knit sweaters, and much more. Processing has this flexibility because of its system of libraries.

A Processing *library* is a collection of code that extends the software beyond its core functions and classes. Libraries have been important to the growth of the project, because they let developers add new features quickly. As smaller, self-contained projects, libraries are easier to manage than if these features were integrated into the main software.

To use a library, select Import Library from the Sketch menu and select the library you want to use from the list. Choosing a library adds a line of code that indicates that the library will be used with the current sketch.

For instance, when the PDF Export Library (pdf) is added, this line of code is added to the top of the sketch:

```
add_library('pdf')
```

In addition to the libraries included with Processing (these are called the *core* libraries), there are over 100 *contributed* libraries that are linked from the Processing website. All libraries are listed online at *http://processing.org/reference/libraries/*.

Before a contributed library can be imported through the Sketch menu, it must be added through the *Library Manager*. Select the Import Library option from the Sketchbook menu and then select Add Library to open the Library Manager interface. Click on a library description and then click on the Install button to download it to your computer.

The downloaded files are saved to the *libraries* folder that is located in your sketchbook. You can find the location of your sketchbook by opening the Preferences. The Library Manager can also be used to update and remove libraries.

As mentioned before, there are more than 100 Processing libraries, so they clearly can't all be discussed here. We've selected a few that we think are fun and useful to introduce in this chapter.

Sound

The *Sound audio library* introduced with Processing 3.0 has the ability to play, analyze, and generate (synthesize) sound. This library needs to be downloaded with the Library Manager as described earlier. (It's not included with the main Processing download because of its size.)

Like the images, shape files, and fonts introduced in Chapter 7, a sound file is another type of media to augment a Processing sketch. Processing's Sound library can load a range of file formats including WAV, AIFF, and MP3. Once a sound file is loaded, it can be played, stopped, and looped, or even distorted using different "effects" classes.

Example 13-1: Play a Sample

The most common use of the Sound library is to play a sound as background music or when an event happens on screen. The following example builds on Example 8-5 on page 103 to play a sound when the shape hits the edges of the screen. The *blip.wav* file is included in the *media* folder that can be downloaded by following the instructions in Chapter 7.

As with other media, the variable that will contain the SoundFile object is defined at the top of the sketch, it's loaded within setup(), and after that, it can be used anywhere in the program:

```
add_library('sound')

blip = None
radius = 120
x = 0
speed = 1.0
direction = 1

def setup():
    global blip, x
    size(440, 440)
    ellipseMode(RADIUS)
    blip = SoundFile(this, "blip.wav")
    x = width/2 # Start in the center

def draw():
    global x, direction
    background(0)
    x += speed * direction
    if x > width-radius or x < radius:
        direction = -direction # Flip direction
        blip.play()
    if direction == 1:
        arc(x, 220, radius, radius, 0.52, 5.76) # Face right
    else:
        arc(x, 220, radius, radius, 3.67, 8.9) # Face left
```

The sound is triggered each time its play() method is run. This example works well because the sound is only played when the value of the x variable is at the edges of the screen. If the sound were played each time through draw(), the sound would restart 60 times each second and wouldn't have time to finish playing.

The result is a rapid clipping sound. To play a longer sample while a program runs, call the `play()` or `loop()` method for that sound inside `setup()` so the sound is triggered only a single time.

 The `SoundFile` class has many methods to control how a sound is played. The most essential are `play()` to play the sample a single time, `loop()` to play it from beginning to end over and over, `stop()` to halt the playback, and `jump()` to move to a specific moment within the file.

Example 13-2: Listen to a Microphone

In addition to playing a sound, Processing can listen. If your computer has a microphone, the Sound Library can read live audio through it. Sounds from the mic can be analyzed, modified, and played:

```
add_library('sound')

mic = None
amp = None

def setup():
    global mic, amp
    size(440, 440)
    background(0)
```

```
# Create an audio input and start it
mic = AudioIn(this, 0)
mic.start()
# Create a new amplitude analyzer and patch into input
amp = Amplitude(this)
amp.input(mic)

def draw():
    # Draw a background that fades to black
    noStroke()
    fill(26, 76, 102, 10)
    rect(0, 0, width, height)
    # The analyze() method returns values between 0 and 1,
    # so map() is used to convert the values to larger numbers
    diameter = map(amp.analyze(), 0, 1, 10, width)
    # Draw the circle based on the volume
    fill(255)
    ellipse(width/2, height/2, diameter, diameter)
```

There are two parts to getting the *amplitude* (volume) from an attached microphone. The `AudioIn` class is used to get the signal data from the mic and the `Amplitude` class is used to measure the signal. Objects from both classes are defined at the top of the code and created inside `setup()`.

After the `Amplitude` object (named `amp` here) is made, the `AudioIn` object (named `mic`) is patched in to the `amp` object with the `input()` method. After that, the `analyze()` method of the `amp` object can be run at any time to read the amplitude of the microphone data within the program. In this example, that is done each time through `draw()` and that value is then used to set the size of the circle.

In addition to playing a sound and analyzing sound as demonstrated in the last two examples, Processing can synthesize sound directly. The fundamentals of sound synthesis are waveforms that include the sine wave, triangle wave, and square wave.

A sine wave sounds smooth, a square wave is harsh, and a triangle wave is somewhere between. Each wave has a number of properties. The *frequency*, measured in hertz, determines the pitch—the highness or lowness of the tone. The *amplitude* of the wave determines the volume—the degree of loudness.

Example 13-3: Create a Sine Wave

In the following example, the value of mouseX determines the frequency of a sine wave. As the mouse moves left and right, the audible frequency and corresponding wave visualization increase and decrease:

 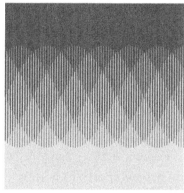

```
add_library('sound')

sine = None
freq = 400.0

def setup():
    global sine
    size(440, 440)
    # Create and start the sine oscillator
    sine = SinOsc(this)
    sine.play()

def draw():
    background(176, 204, 176)
    # Map the mouseX value from 20Hz to 440Hz for frequency
    hertz = map(mouseX, 0, width, 20.0, 440.0)
    sine.freq(hertz)
    # Draw a wave to visualize the frequency of the sound
    stroke(26, 76, 102)
    for x in range(width):
        angle = map(x, 0, width, 0, TWO_PI * hertz)
        sinValue = sin(angle) * 120
        line(x, 0, x, height/2 + sinValue)
```

The `sine` object, created from the `SinOsc` class, is defined at the top of the code and then created inside `setup()`. Like working with a sample, the wave needs to be played with the `play()` method to start generating the sound. Within `draw()`, the `freq()` method continuously sets the frequency of the waveform based on the left-right position of the mouse.

Image and PDF Export

The animated images created by a Processing program can be turned into a file sequence with the `saveFrame()` function. When `saveFrame()` appears at the end of `draw()`, it saves a numbered sequence of TIFF-format images of the program's output named *screen-0001.tif*, *screen-0002.tif*, and so on to the sketch's folder.

These files can be imported into a video or animation program and saved as a movie file. You can also specify your own file-name and image file format with a line of code like this:

```
saveFrame("output-####.png")
```

Use the # (hash mark) symbol to show where the numbers will appear in the filename. They are replaced with the actual frame numbers when the files are saved. You can also specify a sub-folder to save the images into, which is helpful when working with many image frames:

```
saveFrame("frames/output-####.png")
```

 When using `saveFrame()` inside `draw()`, a new file is saved each frame—so watch out, as this can quickly fill your *sketch* folder with thousands of files.

Example 13-4: Saving Images

This example shows how to save images by storing enough frames for a two-second animation. It loads and moves the robot file from "Robot 5: Media" on page 97. See Chapter 7 for instructions for downloading the file and adding it to the sketch.

The example runs the program at 30 frames per second and then exits after 60 frames:

```
bot = None
x = 0

def setup():
    global bot
    size(720, 480)
    bot = loadShape("robot1.svg")
    frameRate(30)

def draw():
    global x
    background(0, 153, 204)
    translate(x, 0)
    shape(bot, 0, 80)
    saveFrame("frames/SaveExample-####.tif")
    x += 12
    if frameCount == 60:
        exit()
```

Processing will write an image based on the file extension that you use (*.png*, *.jpg*, and *.tif* are all built in, and some platforms may support others). A *.tif* image is saved uncompressed, which is fast but takes up a lot of disk space. Both *.png* and *.jpg* will create smaller files, but because of the compression, will usually require more time to save, making the sketch run slowly.

If your desired output is vector graphics, you can write the output to PDF files for higher resolution. The PDF Export library makes it possible to write PDF files directly from a sketch. These vector graphics files can be scaled to any size without losing resolution, which makes them ideal for print output—from posters and banners to entire books.

Example 13-5: Draw to a PDF

This example builds on Example 13-4 on page 185 to draw more robots, but it removes the motion. The PDF library is imported at the top of the sketch to extend Processing to be able to write PDF files.

This sketch creates a PDF file called *Ex-13-5.pdf* because of the third and fourth parameters to size():

```
add_library('pdf')

bot = None

def setup():
  global bot
  size(600, 800, PDF, "Ex-13-5.pdf")
  bot = loadShape("robot1.svg")

def draw():
  background(255)
  for i in range(100):
    rx = random(-bot.width, width)
    ry = random(-bot.height, height)
    shape(bot, rx, ry)
  exit()
```

The geometry is not drawn on the screen; it is written directly into the PDF file, which is saved into the sketch's folder. The code in this example runs once and then exits at the end of draw(). The resulting output is shown in Figure 13-1.

There are more PDF Export examples included with the Processing software. Look in the *PDF Export* (pdf) section of the Processing examples to see more techniques.

Figure 13-1. *PDF export from Example 13-5*

Hello, Arduino

Arduino is an electronics prototyping platform with a series of microcontroller boards and the software to program them. Processing and Arduino share a long history together; they are sister projects with many similar ideas and goals, though they address separate domains. Because they share the same editor and programming environment and a similar syntax, it's easy to move between them and to transfer knowledge about one into the other.

In this section, we focus on reading data into Processing from an Arduino board and then visualizing that data on screen. This makes it possible to use new inputs into Processing programs and to allow Arduino programmers to see their sensor input as graphics. These new inputs can be anything that attaches to an Arduino board. These devices range from a distance sensor to a compass or a mesh network of temperature sensors.

This section assumes that you have an Arduino board and a basic working knowledge of how to use it. If not, you can learn more online at *http://www.arduino.cc* and in the excellent book *Getting Started with Arduino* by Massimo Banzi (Maker Media). Once you've covered the basics, you can learn more about sending data between Processing and Arduino in another outstanding book, *Making Things Talk* by Tom Igoe (Maker Media).

Data can be transferred between a Processing sketch and an Arduino board with some help from the Processing Serial Library. *Serial* is a data format that sends one byte at a time. In the world of Arduino, a *byte* is a data type that can store values between 0 and 255; it works like an `int`, but with a much smaller range. Larger numbers are sent by breaking them into a list of bytes and then reassembling them later.

In the following examples, we focus on the Processing side of the relationship and keep the Arduino code simple. We visualize the data coming in from the Arduino board one byte at a time. With the techniques covered in this book and the hundreds of Arduino examples online, we hope this will be enough to get you started.

Example 13-6: Read a Sensor

The following Arduino code is used with the next three Processing examples:

```
// Note: This is code for an Arduino board, not Processing

int sensorPin = 0;  // Select input pin
int val = 0;

void setup() {
  Serial.begin(9600);  // Open serial port
}

void loop() {
  val = analogRead(sensorPin) / 4;  // Read value from sensor
  Serial.write((byte)val);  // Print variable to serial port
  delay(100);  // Wait 100 milliseconds
}
```

There are two important details to note about this Arduino example. First, it requires attaching a sensor into the analog input on pin 0 on the Arduino board. You might use a light sensor (also called a photo resistor, photocell, or light-dependent resistor) or another analog resistor such as a thermistor (temperature-sensitive resistor), flex sensor, or pressure sensor (force-sensitive resistor). The circuit diagram and drawing of the breadboard with components are shown in Figure 13-2. Next, notice that the value returned by the analogRead() function is divided by 4 before it's assigned to val. The values from analog Read() are between 0 and 1023, so we divide by 4 to convert them to the range of 0 to 255 so that the data can be sent in a single byte.

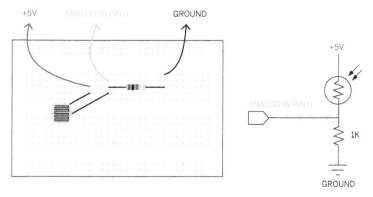

Figure 13-2. *Attaching a light sensor (photo resistor) to analog in pin 0*

Example 13-7: Read Data from the Serial Port

The first visualization example shows how to read the serial data in from the Arduino board and how to convert that data into the values that fit to the screen dimensions:

```
add_library('serial')
port = None  # for object from Serial class
val = 0.0    # Data received from the serial port

def setup():
  global port
  size(440, 220);
  # IMPORTANT NOTE:
  # The first serial port retrieved by Serial.list()
  # should be your Arduino. If not, uncomment the next
  # line by deleting the # before it. Run the sketch
  # again to see a list of serial ports. Then, change
  # the 0 in between [ and ] to the number of the port
  # that your Arduino is connected to.
  #print Serial.list()
  arduinoPort = Serial.list()[0]
  port = Serial(this, arduinoPort, 9600)

def draw():
  global val
  if port.available() > 0:      # If data is available,
    val = port.read()           # read it and store it in val
    val = map(val, 0, 255, 0, height) # Convert the value
  rect(40, val-10, 360, 20)
```

The Serial library is imported on the first line and the serial port is opened in **setup()**. It may or may not be easy to get your Processing sketch to talk with the Arduino board; it depends on your hardware setup. There is often more than one device that the Processing sketch might try to communicate with. If the code doesn't work the first time, read the comment in **setup()** carefully and follow the instructions.

Within **draw()**, the value is brought into the program with the **read()** method of the Serial object. The program reads the data from the serial port only when a new byte is available. The **available()** method checks to see if a new byte is ready and returns the number of bytes available. This program is written so that a single new byte will be read each time through `draw()`. The `map()` function converts the incoming value from its initial range from 0 to 255 to a range from 0 to the height of the screen; in this program, it's from 0 to 220.

Example 13-8: Visualizing the Data Stream

Now that the data is coming through, we'll visualize it in a more interesting format. The values coming in directly from a sensor are often erratic, and it's useful to smooth them out by averaging them. Here, we present the raw signal from the light sensor illustrated in the top half of the example and the smoothed signal in the bottom half:

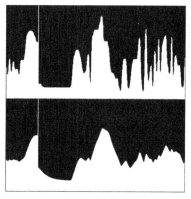
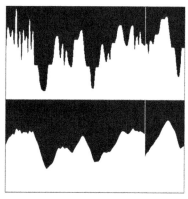

```
add_library('serial')
port = None # for Serial object
val = 0.0    # Data received from the serial port
x = 0
easing = 0.05
easedVal = 0.0

def setup():
  global port
  size(440, 440)
  frameRate(30)
  arduinoPort = Serial.list()[0]
  port = Serial(this, arduinoPort, 9600)
  background(0)

def draw():
```

```
global x, val, easedVal
if port.available() > 0:      # If data is available,
  val = port.read()           # read it and store it in val
  val = map(val, 0, 255, 0, height) # Convert the values
targetVal = val;
easedVal += (targetVal - easedVal) * easing

stroke(0)
line(x, 0, x, height)         # Black line
stroke(255)
line(x+1, 0, x+1, height)     # White line
line(x, 220, x, val)          # Raw value
line(x, 440, x, easedVal + 220) # Averaged value

x += 1
if x > width:
  x = 0
```

Similar to Example 5-8 on page 52 and Example 5-9 on page 53, this sketch uses the easing technique. Each new byte from the Arduino board is set as the target value, the difference between the current value and the target value is calculated, and the current value is moved closer to the target. Adjust the easing variable to affect the amount of smoothing applied to the incoming values.

Example 13-9: Another Way to Look at the Data

This example is inspired by radar display screens. The values are read in the same way from the Arduino board, but they are visualized in a circular pattern using the sin() and cos() functions introduced earlier in Example 8-12 on page 111 to Example 8-15 on page 113:

```
add_library('serial')

port = None   # Serial class object
val = 0.0     # Data received from the serial port
angle = 0.0
radius = 0.0

def setup():
  global port
  size(440, 440)
  frameRate(30)
  strokeWeight(2)
  arduinoPort = Serial.list()[0]
  port = Serial(this, arduinoPort, 9600)
  background(0)

def draw():
  global val, angle, radius
  if port.available() > 0:  # If data is available,
    val = port.read()       # read it and store it in val
    # Convert the values to set the radius
    radius = map(val, 0, 255, 0, height * 0.45)

  middleX = width/2
  middleY = height/2
  x = middleX + cos(angle) * height/2
  y = middleY + sin(angle) * height/2
  stroke(0)
  line(middleX, middleY, x, y)

  x = middleX + cos(angle) * radius
  y = middleY + sin(angle) * radius
```

```
stroke(255)
line(middleX, middleY, x, y)

angle += 0.01
```

The **angle** variable is updated continuously to move the line drawing the current value around the circle, and the **val** variable scales the length of the moving line to set its distance from the center of the screen. After one time around the circle, the values begin to write on top of the previous data.

We're excited about the potential of using Processing and Arduino together to bridge the world of software and electronics. Unlike the examples printed here, the communication can be bidirectional. Elements on screen can also affect what's happening on the Arduino board. This means you can use a Processing program as an interface between your computer and motors, speakers, lights, cameras, sensors, and almost anything else that can be controlled with an electrical signal. Again, check out http://www.arduino.cc for more information about Arduino.

A/Coding Tips

Coding is a type of writing. Like all types of writing, code has specific rules. For comparison, we'll quickly mention some of the rules for English that you probably haven't thought about in a while because they are second nature. Some of the more invisible rules are writing from left to right and putting a space between each word. More overt rules are spelling conventions, capitalizing the names of people and places, and using punctuation at the end of sentences to provide emphasis! If we break one or more of these rules when writing an email to a friend, the message still gets through. For example, "hello ben. how r u today" communicates nearly as well as, "Hello, Ben. How are you today?" However, flexibility with the rules of writing don't transfer to programming. Because you're writing to communicate with a computer, rather than another person, you need to be more precise and careful. One misplaced character is often the difference between a program that runs and one that doesn't.

Processing tries to tell you where you've made mistakes and to guess what the mistake is. When you press the Run button, if there are grammar (syntax) problems with your code (we call them *bugs*), then the Message Area turns red and Processing tries to highlight the line of code that it suspects as the problem. The line of code with the bug is often one line above or below the highlighted line, though in some cases, it's nowhere close. The text in the Message Area tries to be helpful and suggests the potential problem, but sometimes the message is too cryptic to understand. For a beginner, these error messages can be frustrating. Understand that Processing is a simple piece of software that's trying to be helpful, but it has a limited knowledge of what you're trying to do.

Long error messages are printed to the Console in more detail, and sometimes scrolling through that text can offer a hint. Additionally, Processing can find only one bug at a time. If your program has many bugs, you'll need to keep running the program and fix them one at a time.

Please read and reread the following suggestions carefully to help you write clean code.

Functions and Parameters

Programs are composed of many small parts, which are grouped together to make larger structures. We have a similar system in English: words are grouped into phrases, which are combined to make sentences, which are combined to create paragraphs. The idea is the same in code, but the small parts have different names and behave differently. *Functions* and *parameters* are two important parts. Functions are the basic building blocks of a Processing program. Parameters are values that define how the function behaves.

Consider a function like `background()`. Like the name suggests, it's used to set the background color of the Display Window. The function has three parameters that define the color. These numbers define the red, green, and blue components of the color to define the composite color. For example, the following code draws a blue background:

```
background(51, 102, 153)
```

Look carefully at this single line of code. The key details are the parentheses after the function name that enclose the numbers, and the commas between each number. All of these parts need to be there for the code to run. Compare the previous example line to these two broken versions of the same line:

```
background 51, 102, 153 # Error! Missing the parentheses
background(51 102, 153) # Error! Missing a comma
```

The computer is very unforgiving about even the smallest omission or deviation from what it's expecting. If you remember these parts, you'll have fewer bugs. But if you forget to type them, which we all do, it's not a problem. Processing will alert you about the problem, and when it's fixed, the program will run well.

Color Coding

The Processing Development Environment color-codes different parts of each program. Words that are a part of Processing are drawn as blue and orange to distinguish them from the parts of the program that you invent. The words that are unique to your program, such as your variable and function names, are drawn in black. Basic symbols such as ( ), [ ], and > are also black.

Comments

Comments are notes that you write to yourself (or other people) inside the code. You should use them to clarify what the code is doing in plain language and provide additional information such as the title and author of the program. A comment starts with a pound symbol (#) and continues until the end of the line:

```
# This is a comment
```

When a comment is correctly typed, the color of the text will turn gray. The entire commented area turns gray so you can clearly see where it begins and ends.

Uppercase and Lowercase

Python distinguishes uppercase letters from lowercase letters and therefore reads "Hello" as a distinct word from "hello". If you're trying to draw a rectangle with the `rect()` function and you write `Rect()`, the code won't run. You can see if Processing recognizes your intended code by checking the color of the text.

Style

Python is somewhat flexible about how much space is used to format your code. Python doesn't care if you write:

```
rect(50, 20, 30, 40)
```

or:

```
rect (50,20,30,40)
```

or even:

```
rect    (      50,20,30,  40)
```

However, Python uses spaces at the *beginning* of lines (known as "indentation") to determine the structure of your program. For this reason, you need to use indentation carefully when you're writing Python programs. For example, this code will work:

```
for i in range(10):
    square = i * i
    print square
```

But this code will not (notice how the line beginning with **print** has one fewer space than the previous line):

```
for i in range(10):
    square = i * i
   print square
```

It's in your best interest to make the code easy to read. This becomes especially important as the code grows in length. Clean formatting makes the structure of the code immediately legible, and sloppy formatting often obscures problems. Get into the habit of writing clean code. Python has an informal style guide that is used by many programmers called PEP8, which has good ideas for how to format your code. You can read it here: *https://www.python.org/dev/peps/pep-0008/*.

Console

The Console is the bottom area of the Processing Development Environment. You can write messages to the Console with the **print** statement. For example, the following code prints a message followed by the current time:

```
print "Hello, Processing."
print "The time is " + str(hour()) + ":" + str(minute())
```

The Console is essential to seeing what is happening inside of your programs while they run. It's used to print the value of variables so you can track them in order to confirm if events are happening and to determine where a program is having a problem.

One Step at a Time

We recommend writing a few lines of code at a time and running the code frequently to make sure that bugs don't accumulate without your knowledge. Every ambitious program is written one line at a time. Break your project into simpler subprojects and complete them one at a time so that you can have many small successes, rather than a swarm of bugs. If you have a bug, try to isolate the area of the code where you think the problem lies. Try to think of fixing bugs as solving a mystery or puzzle. If you get stuck or frustrated, take a break to clear your head or ask a friend for help. Sometimes, the answer is right under your nose but requires a second opinion to make it clear.

B/Data Types

There are different categories of data. For instance, think about the data on an ID card. The card has numbers to store weight, height, date of birth, street address, and postal code. It has words to store a person's name and city. There's also image data (a photo), and often an organ donor choice, which is a yes/no decision. In Processing, we have different data types to store each kind of data. Each of the following types is explained in more detail elsewhere in the book, but this is a summary:

Name	Description
int	Integers (whole numbers)
float	Floating-point values
bool	Logical value
str	Sequence of characters
PImage	PNG, JPG, or GIF image
PFont	Use the createFont() function or the Create Font tool to make fonts to use with Processing
PShape	SVG file

As a guideline, a **float** number has about four digits of accuracy after the decimal point. If you're counting or taking small steps, you should use an **int** value to take the steps, and then perhaps scale it by a **float** if necessary when putting it to use.

Python automatically determines the data type of a value when you first create it. You can use the built-in **type()** function to check the type of a value or variable. This can be helpful when debugging. For example:

```
x = 10
print type(x) # prints <type 'int'>
y = 17.4
print type(y) # prints <type 'float'>
```

There are more data types than those mentioned here, but these are the most useful for the work typically made with Processing. In fact, as mentioned in Chapter 10, there are infinite types of data, because every new class is a different data type.

C/Order of Operations

When mathematical calculations are performed in a program, each operation takes place according to a prespecified order. This *order of operations* ensures that the code is run the same way every time. This is no different from arithmetic or algebra, but programming has other operators that are less familiar.

In the following table, the operators on the top are evaluated before the operators later in the list—e.g., multiplication will be evaluated before addition.

Name	Symbol	Examples
Parentheses	()	a * (b + c)
Unary negation	-	-x
Multiplicative	* / %	a * b
Additive	+ -	a + b
Comparisons	> < <= >= == != in	if a > b
Logical NOT	not	if not mousePressed
Logical AND	and	if mousePressed and (a > b)
Logical OR	or	if mousePressed or(a > b)

D/Variable Scope

The rule of variable scope in Python is defined simply: a variable created inside a function exists only inside that function. This means that a variable created inside setup() can be used only within setup(), and likewise, a variable declared inside draw() can be used only inside draw(). The exception to this rule is a variable declared outside of setup() and draw(). These variables can be used in both setup() and draw() (or inside any other function that you create). We call these variables *global variables*, because they can be used anywhere within the program. We call a variable that is used only within a single function a *local variable*. Following are a couple of code examples that further explain the concept. First:

```
i = 12   # Assign value 12 to global variable i

def setup():
  size(480, 320)
  i = 24 # Assign value 24 to local variable i
  print i # Prints 24 to the console

def draw():
  print i # Prints 12 to the console
```

And second:

```
def setup():
  size(480, 320)
  i = 24 # Assign 24 to local variable i

def draw():
    print i # ERROR! The variable i is local to setup()
```

As you can see from the initial example, if you make an assignment to a variable inside a function that has the same name as a global variable, Python assumes that you wanted to create a new (local) variable with the same name. If you wanted instead to *change* the value of the global variable, you need to declare this variable as global at the beginning of the function using the **global** keyword:

```
i = 12    # Assign value 12 to global variable i

def setup():
    global i # "i" now means the global variable, not a new local
    size(480, 320)
    i = 24 # Assign value 24 to global variable i
    print i # Prints 24 to the console

def draw():
    print i # Prints 24 to the console
```

You need to use the **global** keyword for any kind of assignment, including the incrementation shortcut operator. Here's an example to illustrate:

```
x = 0

def setup():
    size(200, 200)

def draw():
    background(0)
    stroke(255)
    x += 1
    ellipse(x, 100, 15, 15)
```

The preceding code gives an error when you try to run it ("local variable 'x' referenced before assignment"). That's because we never told Python that we want x inside of the **draw()** function to refer to the global variable x. As a consequence, when we try to increment the value of x, Python doesn't know what we mean, as we never created a variable with that name inside of **draw()**! We can fix the problem by adding **global** at the beginning of the function:

```
x = 0

def setup():
    size(200, 200)

def draw():
    global x
    background(0)
    stroke(255)
```

```
x += 1
ellipse(x, 100, 15, 15)
```

Note that the `global` keyword is needed only when you're planning to *overwrite* the value assigned to a variable. You don't need to use the `global` keyword when performing operations that merely change the object's internal state. To illustrate, in the following example, you don't need to use the `global` keyword, as the value of the variable x (i.e., the list) is not being overwritten. We're merely calling a method on that object and assigning to one of its indexes. (The `global` keyword would be needed, however, if we wanted to create an entirely *new* list and assign it to the same variable x.)

```
x = []
def setup():
  size(600, 200)
  frameRate(5)

def draw():
  background(0)
  noStroke()
  x.append(random(width))
  fill(255, 16)
  for i in range(len(x) - 1):
    ellipse(x[i], height/2, 25, 25)
  fill(255)
  ellipse(x[-1], height/2, 25, 25)
```

E/Processing, Python, and Java

The core Processing project is written in the Java programming language. Processing.py, the flavor of Processing used in this book, allows you to write Processing programs in Python, but is otherwise very closely based on this original Java implementation. A special version of Python (called Jython) is used internally by Processing.py as a "bridge" that allows for direct access to the Processing classes and functions implemented in Java.

For most uses, this integration is seamless. If it's something that Python can do, or if it's something that the Java implementation of Processing can do, you can do it in Processing.py. But you might occasionally encounter a hiccup or two. This appendix describes a few things to look out for as you continue your exploration of Processing and Python.

Python Versions

First off, we should talk about what versions of Python are supported by Processing.py. There are two versions of Python in common use: Python 2 and Python 3. The two versions are very similar, but Python 3 has a number of changes in both syntax and functionality that make it incompatible with previous versions.

Although Python 3 has been available for a number of years, Python 2 remains popular, and many if not most of the Python tutorials and example programs you're likely to find on the Internet are written with Python 2 in mind. Processing.py itself uses Python 2 internally (in particular, it uses a custom build of Jython 2.5, which is largely compatible with Python 2.7). Keep this in mind when consulting documentation and code samples.

Built-In Function Names

There are a number of built-in Processing functions that share the same name as built-in Python functions. Processing.py does a good job of automatically deciding which of these functions to use, based on the number and kind of parameters passed to the function. But you may occasionally find yourself on the receiving end of error messages or strange behavior when using these functions. The trickiest of these functions are listed here, along with a description of how Processing.py decides which version of the function to call:

`set()`

> The Python built-in function with this name returns a new set object. This function will be called in Processing.py if you provide it with zero parameters or one parameter. Otherwise, the Processing built-in function will be called, which sets a pixel at a particular coordinate on the screen to the given color.

`map()`

> This is a Python built-in function that creates a new list by applying a function call to each item in the list. In Processing, this is a linear interpolation function. If your call to the function has five numeric parameters, Processing.py will call the Processing built-in function; otherwise, the Python built-in will be called.

`filter()`

> In Python, this built-in function creates a copy of a list including only those members for which a given test evaluates to true. In Processing, this is a built-in function that processes on-screen pixels. The Processing version is called if supplied with one or two numeric parameters (including Processing constants identifying filter modes); the Python version is called otherwise.

Colors

Some Processing programmers may be accustomed to specifying colors using a pound symbol, like so: #003399. This syntax does not work in Processing.py. Instead, you can pass a string literal with the same notation to any Processing function that accepts a color. For example:

```
fill("#003399")
stroke("#FFFFFF")
rect(10, 10, 80, 80)
```

Python Standard Library

Because Processing.py is just Python under the hood, you can use any module included in Python's standard library. We took advantage of this fact to use the `csv` and `json` libraries in Chapter 12. Using a module in the standard library is easy: simply include an `import` statement at the beginning of your source code. For example, to use the Python `datetime` library:

```
import datetime
# print the current time in ISO8601 format
print datetime.datetime.utcnow().isoformat()
```

You can find a full list of libraries included with Python here: https://docs.python.org/2.7/library/index.html.

Note that the Python `random` library shares the same name as the Processing built-in function `random`. If you import Python's `random` library, it will make the Processing `random` function unavailable in your program.

Processing Libraries and Example Code

The Java implementation of Processing has many helpful libraries, including hundreds of libraries contributed by volunteers and community members. One of the benefits of Processing.py's Java-based implementation is that most of these libraries will work in your program with little or no modification.

But there's a problem: you're likely to find that most Processing libraries you come across have example code for Java Processing only. Fortunately, it's usually possible to translate simple Java examples to Python with a little bit of know-how and effort.

To demonstrate, here's the Java example program for Nikolaus Gradwohl's `ttslib` library, which makes it easy to add text-tospeech to your Processing sketch. (You can download this library in the Processing IDE by selecting Sketch → Import Library... → Add Library... and then searching for "ttslib" in the Library Manager.) We've annotated the code with comments about what needs to be changed to make the example work in Processing.py.

```
import guru.ttslib.*; // use add_library() instead of import

TTS tts; // don't need to include class type ("TTS")

void setup() { // change to def setup():
  tts = new TTS(); // don't need to use "new" keyword in Python
}

void draw() { // change to def draw():
} // use Python "pass" keyword here to replace empty curly
brackets

void mousePressed() { // change to def mousePressed():
  tts.speak("Hi! I am a speaking Processing sketch");
}
```

Here's the equivalent code in Python:

```
add_library('ttslib')

tts = None

def setup():
  global tts
  tts = TTS()

def draw():
  pass

def mousePressed():
  tts.speak("Hi! I am a Processing dot pie sketch")
```

Many Processing libraries (including the sound library introduced in "Sound" on page 180) require a reference to the current PApplet object. In the Java implementation of Processing, you can use the **this** keyword for this purpose. Python, however, doesn't have a built-in **this** keyword, so Processing.py automatically provides a global variable called **this** that you can pass to libraries that require it.

Index

Symbols

* (asterisk), multiplication operator, 38, 205
: (colon)
  in for loops, 40
  in if blocks, 56
{} (curly braces), enclosing JSON
  objects, 168-169
= (equal sign), assignment operator, 38, 205
== (equal sign, double), equal to
  operator, 56-57, 61, 205
!= (exclamation point, equal sign),
  not equal to operator, 61, 205
< (left angle bracket), less than
  operator, 61, 205
<= (left angle bracket, equal sign),
  less than or equal operator, 61,
  205
- (minus sign), subtraction operator, 38, 205
(number sign)
  indicating comments, 30-31
  preceding color values, 212
() (parentheses), in expressions,
  39, 205
. (period), dot operator, 136
+ (plus sign), addition operator, 38,
  205
> (right angle bracket), greater
  than operator, 61, 205
>= (right angle bracket, equal
  sign), greater than or equal
  operator, 61, 205
/ (slash), division operator, 38, 205
[] (square brackets)
  chaining, 175-176

enclosing dictionary keys,
  156-157
enclosing list values, 144, 145

A

add_library() function, 180
AIFF files, 180
alpha value, 27
ALT value, 67
and operator, 63, 67, 205
animation, 99
  bouncing off screen edges,
    103-104
  circular movement, 109-114
  frames, 99-100
  moving randomly, 105-107
  moving shapes, 100-104
  moving with tweening, 104-105
  robot using, 114
  saving as images, 185-186
  timed movement, 108
  wrapping around screen,
    101-103
APIs, accessing network data with,
  172-176
append() method, 144, 146
applications, exporting sketches
  as, 11
arc() function, 18-19
Arduino platform, 188-195
  reading a sensor, 189-190
  reading from serial port, 191-192
  visualizing data from, 192-195
arithmetic operators, 37-39, 205
arrays (see lists)
arrow keys, 67
arrow shape, 28-29
asterisk (*), multiplication operator, 38, 205

B

background() function, 25, 26, 50
Banzi, Massimo (Getting Started with Arduino), 189
beginShape() function, 28
bool data type, 203
boolean data type, 55
bouncing shapes off screen edges, 103-104

C

case sensitivity, 199
circles
    detecting whether cursor is within, 61-62
    drawing, 10
circular movement, 109-114
classes, 131-135
    (see also objects)
    creating objects from, 135-137
    fields in, 130, 131
    __init__ method in, 132-134
    methods in, 130, 132, 134-135
code examples
    permission to use, xii-xiii
    in Processing.py window, opening, 12
CODED value, 67
coding (see programming)
colon (:)
    in for loops, 40
    in if blocks, 56
color
    background color, 25, 26, 50
    fill color, 25, 26, 27
    gray values, 25
    outline color, 23, 26
    transparency of, 27
    values of, 23-25, 26, 212
color coding in PDE, 199
Color Selector option, Tools menu, 26
comma-separated values file (see CSV and TSV files)
comments in code, 30-31, 199

comparison operators (see relational operators)
compound data types, 155-156
    (see also dictionaries; lists; objects)
Console, in PDE, 9, 48, 200
contact information for this book, xiv
CONTROL value, 67
conventions used in this book, xii
coordinate system, 13, 73
cos() function, 109-114
createFont() function, 91
createShape() function, 95-96
creature shapes, 29-30
CSV and TSV files, 162-168
    data types in, handling, 163-164
    header row in, 166-168
    reading data from, 162-163
    reading data into dictionaries, 166-168
    reading data into lists, 164-166
    robot using, 176-178
csv library, 162
curly braces ({}), enclosing JSON objects, 168-169
cursor, location of, 59-64

D

data (see CSV and TSV files; dictionaries; JSON files;network data)
data folder, 85-86
data types, 36, 155-156, 203
degrees, 19
dictionaries, 156-157
    checking for keys in, 157
    keys in, 156-158
    lists of, 158-161
    reading CSV data into, 166-168
    reading JSON files into, 169-172
DictReader() function, 167
Display Window, 13-14, 37
dist() function, 51
dots (see points)
DOWN value, 67

About the Authors

Allison Parrish is a computer programmer, poet, educator, and game designer who lives in Brooklyn. She recently completed a two-year term as the Digital Creative Writer-in-Residence at Fordham University and is a long-time adjunct professor at ITP, where she teaches a course on writing computer programs that generate poetry.

Casey Reas is a professor in the Department of Design Media Arts at UCLA and a graduate of the MIT Media Laboratory. His software has been featured in numerous solo and group exhibitions at museums and galleries in the United States, Europe, and Asia. With Ben Fry, he cofounded Processing in 2001. He is the coauthor of *Processing: A Programming Handbook for Visual Designers and Artists* (2007) and *Form+Code in Design, Art, and Architecture* (2010). His work is archived at www.reas.com.

Ben Fry is principal of Fathom, a design and software consultancy located in Boston. He received his PhD from the Aesthetics + Computation Group at the MIT Media Laboratory, where his research focused on combining fields such as computer science, statistics, graphic design, and data visualization as a means for understanding information. Ben cofounded Processing with Casey Reas in 2001.

Colophon

The body typeface is Benton Sans designed by Tobias Frere-Jones and Cyrus Highsmith. The code font is TheSansMono Condensed Regular by Luc(as) de Groot. The display typeface is Serifa designed by Adrian Frutiger.

CPSIA information can be obtained
at www.ICGtesting.com
Printed in the USA
BVOW11s1054140516

447605BV00001B/1/P

9 781457 186837